To: An... From: W. Edmonton 2/11/20

JOHN DEWEY AND THE DECLINE

OF AMERICAN EDUCATION

JOHN DEWEY AND THE DECLINE

OF AMERICAN EDUCATION

How the Patron Saint of Schools Has Corrupted Teaching and Learning

Henry T. Edmondson III

ISI Books
Wilmington, Delaware

Edmondson, Henry T.
    John Dewey and the decline of American education : how the patron saint of schools has corrupted teaching and learning / Henry T. Edmondson III. — 1st ed. — Wilmington, Del. : ISI Books, c2006.

        p. ; cm.
        ISBN-13: 978-1-932236-52-1
        ISBN-10: 1-932236-52-X
        Includes bibliographical references and index.

        1. Dewey, John, 1859-1952—Influence. 2. Educational change—United States. 3. Education—United States—Philosophy. 4. Education—United States—History. I. Title.

LB875.D5 E36 2006   2004104757
370/.1/0973—dc22   0512

Published in the United States by:

    ISI Books
    Intercollegiate Studies Institute
    Post Office Box 4431
    Wilmington, DE 19807-0431

                Interior design by Kara Beer
        Manufactured in the United States of America

CONTENTS

To Teachers

Acknowledgments

THIS PROJECT HAS STRETCHED OVER a long period of time. For that reason, it is impossible to acknowledge fully the long train of those who have lent their support and encouragement. I must be satisfied, then, with mentioning only a few.

Thanks are due to George Carey at Georgetown University for his encouragement a few years back in this project; and, even farther back, to Gene Miller at the University of Georgia for sparking my interest in the educational views of the founders. When I submitted a class paper comparing John Dewey and the founders he was mildly encouraging in his careful manner, admonishing me that this interest held promise but only with "a great deal of work."

Twenty years is all I can give it, Gene.

I'd like to thank Jeremy Beer of ISI Books for his patience and hard work. He has an editorial wisdom beyond his years.

More important is my gratitude to my wife Dorothy Marie for her unfailing love and support.

My children—Nathan, Erin, Jason, and Kerrie—keep my pedagogical feet on the ground, so to speak, and hopefully prevent me, in some measure, from committing the same error of living in the abstract of which I have accused Dewey and his followers.

A thank you is due also to our family and friends who have helped us through recent challenging years and have shown us the true meaning of family and friendship. Without that support, this project would have perhaps died for lack of spirit.

We are especially grateful to my mother, Frances, who also happens to be one of the best middle-school teachers I've had (even if I wasn't the best student). My late father was an excellent teacher in his own right—though, since I broke with family tradition, he never had the opportunity to teach me surgery as I know he would have enjoyed.

I come from a family of teachers—they are everywhere I turn—and my conversations with them have helped me more than they would imagine, whether it is about mainstreaming the emotionally disturbed, challenging the gifted, or validating and managing the parental passions of the disabled.

As always, my department has been supportive through the last few years; I owe a particular debt of gratitude to Mike Digby, Maria Gordon, Paula McBride, and especially Kim Ireland.

Special thanks are due Kevin O'Keefe for introducing me to Jaime Castiello late in this project.

Finally, this undertaking is perhaps the best thanks I can muster to all the teachers throughout my life who have made something a little better of the raw material they've been given.

Works by Dewey Cited in Text

My Pedagogical Creed (Washington, DC: The Progressive Association, 1929 [1897]), cited as PC.

The School and Society (Chicago: University of Chicago Press, 1899), cited as SS.

Moral Principles in Education (Boston: Houghton Mifflin, 1909), cited as MPE.

How We Think (Mineola, NY: Dover, 1997 [1910]), cited as HWT.

Schools of Tomorrow (New York: E. P. Dutton & Company, 1915), cited as ST.

Democracy and Education (New York: Macmillan, 1916), cited as DE.

Human Nature and Conduct: An Introduction to Social Psychology (New York: Henry Holt, 1922), cited as HNC.

Experience and Nature (New York: Dover, 1958 [1925]), cited as EN.

The Public and Its Problems (New York: Henry Holt, 1927), cited as PP.

The Quest for Certainty (New York: Minton, Balch & Company, 1929), cited as QC.

Liberalism and Social Action (New York: G. P. Putnam's Sons, 1935), cited as LSA.

Experience and Education (New York: Macmillan, 1938), cited as EE.

Our Common Faith (New Haven, CT: Yale University Press, 1934), cited as OCF.

Freedom and Culture (New York: G. P. Putnam's Sons, 1939), cited as FC.

The Living Thoughts of Thomas Jefferson (London and Edinburgh: Morrison and Gibb Ltd., 1941), cited as TJ.

Reconstruction in Philosophy (Boston: Beacon Press, 1949), cited as RP.

Preface

"Don't worry, Scout," Jem comforted me. "Our teacher
says Miss Caroline's introducing a new way of teaching.
She learned about it in college. It'll be in all the grades
soon. You don't have to learn much out of books that
way—it's like if you wanta learn about cows, you go milk
one, see?"
— Harper Lee, *To Kill a Mockingbird*

AMERICAN EDUCATION HAS DETERIORATED SINCE the beginning of the twentieth century, a decline especially pronounced since
the 1950s. While most acute in the elementary and secondary
schools, this decline is evident in higher education as well. In April
1983, the Department of Education issued "A Nation at Risk," the
report that made explicit what many already knew anecdotally or
intuitively: American public education had degenerated badly; the
current system fares poorly when compared to the American past
and when compared to the educational systems of other industrialized nations. The report initiated a wave of concern and debate over
educational reform, discussions that have grown ever more intense,
if not better informed. In 1998 a fifteenth-anniversary study, "A
Nation Still At Risk," concluded that very little had changed since
1983. Despite numerous reform efforts, almost every means of
evaluation draws the same conclusion: not only is education not
improving in the United States, it continues to decline.[1]

This decline is usually defined in terms of:

- a steady drop in standardized test scores, especially the Scholastic Aptitude Test (SAT) and the American College Test (ACT);

- the low percentage of high school graduates who are prepared to enter the university without remedial work;

- the widespread necessity of remedial programs at American colleges and universities, programs that have become a fixed and thriving industry in higher education;

- comparative international test scores, especially as measured by the International Association for the Evaluation of Education Achievement (IEA). Moreover, it seems that the further American students advance through elementary and secondary school, the worse they do in comparison with international students;

- various measures of historical and literary knowledge, all of which—almost without exception—reveal abysmal ignorance and illiteracy among U.S. students;

- various indications that students are all too often followed in their academic descent by the very group responsible for teaching them;

- the opinion of many American parents, based on experience, anecdotal evidence, and in some cases intuition, that U.S. schools are failing their children. This opinion is expressed in part by the growing number of parents who opt for private schools, charter schools, or home schools—often at great personal sacrifice;

- measurements indicating that the rate of "functional illiteracy" in the United States is twice that of many other industrialized nations;

- and clear indications that each of the above trends is even more pronounced among many minority communities.

Reform initiatives aimed at addressing these concerns typically attempt to restore academic excellence in our schools by concentrating on one or more of three distinct levels of action. The first is the *constitutional* level, on which reformers must grapple with a long train of Supreme Court opinions, many of which are confusing. These Court decisions have affected, for better or worse, many educational activities, from prayer at the beginning of the day to the bus route taken after the closing bell. The most significant decision in recent years is the Supreme Court's *Zelman v. Simmons-Harris*, announced on July 2, 2002, in which a bare majority of the Court sensibly declared that the school voucher program in Cleveland, Ohio, did *not* violate the establishment clause of the First Amendment, notwithstanding the fact that some parents might redeem those vouchers in "religious" schools.

This decision prompted immediate and intense action on the second level of educational reform effort, the *political* level. Anyone involved in these struggles knows that education politics can be especially vicious. Woodrow Wilson was once asked why he resigned as president of Princeton University in order to run for the U.S. presidency. He explained, "I couldn't stand the politics." Today, powerful educational interest groups, including the National Education Association, the American Federation of Teachers, and their allies in Washington, DC, and the fifty states, have pledged to wage a fierce battle against any Cleveland-type voucher initiatives that communities elsewhere in the country might wish to undertake. Their ostensible motive for doing so is to protect the future of the public school system and especially the interests of poorer families with school-age children, yet most objective observers agree that the NEA and the AFT cannot or will not distinguish between the welfare of students and their own desire to maintain the power and prestige of their respective organizations. The NEA and AFT rightly fear that the power of their organizations will be weakened if the states' education monopolies are broken. The outcome of this political battle is uncertain, largely because it is tied to the overall balance of political forces in the country at large. That is, unless there is a sea change in the political and ideological balance of power, the battle over school vouchers will probably remain in a stalemate for some time. On the other hand, it may well be that this very issue could itself be the catalyst of a significant shift in the political landscape, given the swelling tide of dissatisfaction over the state of American public education.

However, even if the constitutional and the political dimensions of this struggle were to become characterized by sensible and fair-minded debate, practice, and governance, there is no guarantee that education would improve significantly—not if there is insufficient clarity in educational philosophy. This third dimension of reform, the *philosophical* level, has received less attention than the other two, but it may be the most important. Indeed, until the deep flaws in American educational philosophy are confronted, efforts in the political arena, if not the constitutional, are likely to continue to fail. And to the degree that American educational philosophy is unsound, that weakness is largely attributable to the influence of John Dewey, the progressive turn-of-the-century reformer whose impact on American education is incalculable. Yet Dewey's ideas, and their impact on American educational thought, are poorly understood, especially among the very people who run our schools.

Hence this book, the purpose of which is to explicate the principle elements of Dewey's philosophy and to suggest the ways that his work has harmed American education. In doing so, I hope to call attention to the power of ideas in education, a phenomenon insufficiently understood. In Dewey's case, these ideas, often imported into the schools without sufficient consideration, have gone on to undermine and distort American educational philosophy. The result has been the deterioration, confusion, and disarray we see all around us, a situation that will not markedly improve until we acknowledge and understand the intellectual source of our plight.[2]

I

=

Dewey's Troubling Legacy

My advice to all parents is . . . anything that Wm. Heard
Kilpatrick & Jhn. Dewey say do, don't do.
— Flannery O'Connor

JOHN DEWEY'S NINETIETH BIRTHDAY CELEBRATION was an international event. Jay Martin writes, "Salutations arrived from all over the
world. Programs of speeches about Dewey's importance were organized
in Canada, Denmark, England, France, Holland, Israel, Italy, Japan,
Mexico, Norway, Sweden, and Turkey." A three-day symposium was
held in Tokyo; commemorative events were held in Mexico and
Istanbul as well. In the United States, a fund was established to raise
$90,000 to contribute to causes of his choice and a three-day birthday
event was held in New York City in which over "one hundred schools
and learned societies held programs of tribute to Dewey." Dewey, with
characteristic humility, said afterwards that he had been uncomfortable
with all the "fuss and bother."[1]

By all accounts, Dewey was a benevolent man. My interest in
Dewey began in graduate school, and grew out of my interest in the
American founding period. When I came to realize how important the
educational views of the founders were to the success of their political
project, I then turned my attention to Dewey, to try to determine what

his educational revolution meant to the original founding intentions. During that time I was introduced to a member of the faculty at my university, who as a child, had delivered eggs for Dewey, produced on the philosopher's farm in Burlington, Vermont. His memory of Dewey, not surprisingly, was that of a kind, gentle, and patient man.

What, then has happened? How has Dewey become the *bête noire* of traditionalist educational reformers and why do many of his advocates often find themselves in the role of defending him? To be sure, Dewey is not only controversial, but is regarded with antipathy by some, including the individual who, with overblown rhetoric, told me that Dewey is "the Antichrist!" How do we explain this controversial legacy that only seems to grow more intense with each passing year, and with each drop in the academic performance of American students?

The beginning of such an inquiry must be recognition of the extent of Dewey's influence today. Indeed, in this period of crisis in American schools, a sound understanding of the philosophical underpinnings of American education is impossible without a firm grasp of John Dewey's contribution. Although the ideas of Thomas Jefferson, George Washington, Dr. Benjamin Rush, and others of the founding generation still enjoy moderate influence here and there in American schools and universities, the prestige of Dewey's thought has long superseded that of the founders.[2] He remains "a towering figure."[3]

Revivals of Dewey's thought appear at regular intervals, the latest signaled by the completion in 1990 of the thirty-seven-volume compendium of Dewey's works by the University of Southern Illinois Press,[4] a commendable endeavor that has made Dewey's prolific but disparate body of writings more accessible than ever. Additional evidence of continued interest in Dewey's relevance includes the republication of Sidney Hook's 1939 uncritical apologetic for Dewey's thought, *John Dewey: An Intellectual Portrait* (1995), Alan

Ryan's *John Dewey and the High Tide of American Liberalism* (1997), Jennifer Welchman's *Dewey's Ethical Thought* (1995), James Campbell's *Understanding John Dewey: Nature and Cooperative Intelligence* (1995), Robert B. Westbrook's *John Dewey and American Democracy* (1991), and Jay Martin's biography, *The Education of John Dewey* (2003).[5] *Reading Dewey: Interpretations for a Postmodern Generation* offers fresh formulations of Dewey's thought in education, ethics, psychology, and philosophy.[6] One of the boldest uses of Dewey is the educational theorist Alfie Kohn's *The Schools Our Children Deserve: Moving Beyond Traditional Classrooms and "Tougher Standards"* (1999), in which the author employs Dewey to muster resistance to the gravitational pull back to traditional pedagogy.[7] Dewey's influence, especially his romantic views of human nature and his insistence on "community," is also deeply imprinted on another of Kohn's books, *Beyond Discipline: From Compliance to Community* (1996).[8] In a general introduction to Dewey's philosophy, Raymond Boisvert argues that the political, social, economic, and educational challenges of the new millennium give fresh immediacy to Dewey's attempt to construct a new foundation for democracy.[9] Similar appeals are frequently made in the many psychology and educational journals and conferences that populate the academic landscape.

At times, such calls for a revival of Deweyan approaches have a tone of outright reverence. An article on Dewey and moral education employs a telling, if odd, metaphor: "The Crux of Our Inspiration."[10] Sara Lawrence-Lightfoot, in *The Essential Conversation: What Parents and Teachers Can Learn from Each Other* (2003), recommends Dewey's *My Pedagogical Creed* as a "provocative and incisive series of essays" offering "guiding principles about education, teaching and curriculum, child development, and the relationship between school and society."[11] In an appeal for innovative school reform, *Shaking Up the Schoolhouse*, author Phillip Schlechty recommends that education leaders familiarize themselves with "classic" literature "such as the works of Shakespeare and the Bible—and with the writings of profound thinkers in the field of education such as John Dewey, Alfred North Whitehead, and Bertrand Russell."[12] An article in the leading education periodical *Education Week* went so far as to recommend Dewey's ideas as a guide for helping students to assimilate the tragedy of September 11, 2001.[13]

At the same time, there have appeared a few volumes tying Dewey to American educational decline. For example, educational theorist Kieran Egan's *Getting It Wrong from the Beginning* explores the contemporary dominance of progressive education and its deteriorating effect on U.S. schools.[14] In *Left Back: A Century of Battles over School Reform*, respected educational historian Dianne Ravitch notes John Dewey's influence in generating at least two of the misconceptions that now cripple American education: the use of schools to solve social and political problems and the depreciation of academics in favor of assorted "activities."[15] In *Class Warfare: Besieged Schools, Bewildered Parents, Betrayed Kids, and the Attack on Excellence*, political scientist J. Martin Rochester points to Dewey as the source of most contemporary abuses in education policy; and Charles J. Sykes's *Dumbing Down Our Kids* is an exposé of the problems of contemporary education and their source in the progressive education movement.[16]

The Elements of Dewey's Thought

Unfortunately, despite his iconic status, Dewey is rarely read and his work is poorly understood in public schools and in colleges of education. Future teachers often learn a little bit "about" Dewey the man and educator, but they are never given the opportunity to assess critically the Deweyan ideas that underlie their classes and permeate their professional organizations. Educational bureaucrats, activists, and accrediting agencies do not seem to appreciate the source of the ideas that inspire their work, either. Political scientists, who might be expected to have the training and objectivity to furnish a different perspective on Dewey's educational thought, usually concentrate on his political and social philosophy, mostly found in such volumes as *Democracy and Education* (1915), *The Public and Its Problems* (1927), *Liberalism and Social Action* (1935), and *Freedom and Culture* (1939). As a political and social philosopher, Dewey is famous for his advocacy of contemporary liberalism, if not socialism. For instance, he argued for greater government involvement in society at large because our enjoyment of equality depends upon such intervention.[17] In *Human Nature and Conduct* (1922), he contends that freedom is meaningless if government does not actively intervene in the private sector to enable its citizens to enjoy that freedom. Freedom "from oppressive legal and political measures" is not sufficient for the enjoyment of liberty, writes Dewey. What men need is a social "environment" that will help them obtain their "wants" as well as their needs (HNC, 305–6).

This focus on Dewey's social and political philosophy, however, brings only one dimension of his work into view. It neglects Dewey's own assertion that in order to fully appreciate his philosophy it should be read as a complete system. Given the breadth of Dewey's work, this is admittedly a difficult task. Dewey explicitly argues, nonetheless, that all philosophy—like life in general—should be considered as a whole. Focusing only upon artificially delimited aspects of his thought makes it difficult to see the larger picture.

In fact, for the educator and the political scientist alike, studying Dewey's educational philosophy offers a unique advantage, for it is in his educational thought that all the dimensions of his philosophy intersect. In other words, for Dewey, all philosophy is, in a sense, educational philosophy, because it is only in education that all branches of philosophy find their consummation. Education was Dewey's passion, the field in which his political aspirations, moral philosophy, and psychological innovations found their purpose. Indeed, Dewey's instrumentalism teaches precisely that philosophy is so much wasted time and effort if it is not "useful."

Dewey may have hoped to influence intellectual life through other dimensions of his work, but he expected to change the world through his educational thought. In order to do so, he explains in *Democracy and Education*, he must "contend not only with the inertia of existing educational traditions," but also with the opposition of those who control business and government, since they depend upon the educational system to produce workers and citizens (DE, 319). Such philosophical and political reconstruction is essential, Dewey believes, to preserve the American democratic experiment—indeed, to save it from destruction. In order to survive, American democracy must be transformed by a revolution in education, followed by a social and economic revolution. One cannot occur without the other, but education must first be revolutionized because it is "the process through which the needed transformation may be accomplished" (DE, 332).

Dewey is often described as a philosophical pragmatist, a designation he shares with two other American philosophers, William James and Charles Peirce. He acknowledges in the closing pages of *Democracy and Education* that "[t]he theory of the method of knowing which is advanced in these pages may be termed pragmatic" (DE, 344). Dewey argues that education—even more than politics—should promote the practical over the abstract. To pursue change through politics can be frustratingly slow; using education to change the world is far more efficient. The ultimate result of such change is political and social transformation.

Yet, ironically, Dewey's educational system has every appearance of being grossly impractical. The more one reads Dewey, the more one is forced to conclude that his self-styled pragmatism is not so much a "practical" choice as it is a convenient cover for his politics. Dewey's philosophy, then, must always be interpreted in light of his preoccupation with social change. Indeed, in some places Dewey chooses the more militant term "instrumentalism" rather than "pragmatism" to describe his philosophy because the former signals a stance more decidedly opposed to the ideas that retard progress. In his view, traditional notions of human nature, of the structure and process of democracy, and of the nature of truth itself all must be reworked (DE, 331).

Later in his career, Dewey characterized his work as "experimental," and this term may well be the most appropriate of all, since it points to the *anti*-utilitarianism evident in his thought. There are times when Dewey's unrelenting passion for discrediting and demolishing all that is traditional compromises his pragmatism to the point that his philosophy descends to nihilism. Dewey is intent on razing the traditional landscape as a prerequisite to building anew, which is why he is often more concerned with undermining tradition and conventional religion than he is with finding more efficient ways for students to learn.

Indeed, Dewey's thought is characterized by hostility, not only to traditional religion, but to all abstract or metaphysical ideas, even though his own writing is at times irremediably abstract. He argues, for example, that belief in objective truth and authoritative notions of good and evil are harmful to students. Dewey's ostensible rationale for so strongly opposing such ideas is that they are obstacles to students' intellectual and moral growth. Dewey's real opposition, though, may arise from his concern that a belief in objective truth is an impediment to the promulgation of his own philosophical ideas. Indeed, for someone so ostensibly concerned that students think for themselves, Dewey can be surprisingly dogmatic.

It is a commonplace these days for this or that educational reform to be promoted because it is "for the good of students"—and to expect that everyone will accept such a claim at face value. A study of Dewey's thought, however, compels us to be suspicious of this kind of rhetoric. It is not going too far to say that, in the final analysis, Dewey is not most interested in the good of students but rather the successful promotion of a political program. If that political program also happens to be for the academic and moral benefit of students—as he undoubtedly thought it was—then that is a happy coincidence.

Rousseau in the Classroom

The single most important influence on progressive education, both European and American, has been Jean-Jacques Rousseau's educational treatise *Emile*, which was itself a reaction to conventional pedagogy. Dewey, like other reformers, was profoundly influenced by Rousseau. In *Schools of Tomorrow* (1915), Dewey notes approvingly that the eighteenth-century French philosopher is "very recently beginning to enjoy respect" (ST, 290). Some have even hailed Dewey's *Democracy and Education* (1916) as "the most notable contribution to pedagogy since Rousseau's *Emile*."[18] Dewey shares Rousseau's optimistic view that human beings are basically benevolent and human nature is easily molded, and he believes with Rousseau that moral education designed to subdue human nature by overcoming vice is harmful to students. Dewey shares Rousseau's rejection, not only of tradition, but also of conventional religion, although he does not share the private nonconformist religious aspirations to which Rousseau occasionally admitted. Dewey adopts Rousseau's "child-centered" curriculum—as educational reformers would later call it—and he further follows Rousseau's classroom strategy insofar as the curriculum is only *apparently* centered on the child: the child's learning environment is in reality a grand manipulation on the part of his tutor or teacher. Rousseau disdained educational goals and ideals just as Dewey would later do. In both cases, the opposition to such standards is supposedly for the sake of immediacy and relevance in the learning process. For both educators as well, learning largely consists of hands-on experience.

Both Rousseau and Dewey depreciate the importance of books for students, in Rousseau's case at least until well into adolescence. With Dewey, it is not clear when or if books should ever become a primary component of a student's education. Rousseau urges that his student Emile learn a useful trade; Dewey also emphasizes vocational education, primarily because he finds it easy to manage that particular learning experience in the interest of preparing students to be social reformers. Finally, both Dewey's and Rousseau's educational thought is motivated by a belief that education should promote freedom, although neither thinker unambiguously defines what freedom means. Dewey's only serious disagreement with Rousseau has to do with the latter's individualistic educational plan: for Dewey, education must be a predominantly social experience.

In *Schools of Tomorrow*, Dewey concedes that "Rousseau said, as well as did, many foolish things," but he nevertheless finds Rousseau to be an inspirational figure, judging by the prominence the French philosopher enjoys in that book (ST, 1). Dewey does, however, acknowledge an embarrassing fact of Rousseau's legacy. He writes, "Rousseau, while he was writing his *Emile*, was allowing his own children to grow up entirely neglected by their parents, abandoned in a foundling asylum" (ST, 60). Rousseau's life thus highlights an uncomfortable fact about progressive educational reform through the past decades: there often exists a disturbing split between abstract theory and actual experience. For an idea to be considered "good," it is not necessary that its proponent has actually practiced it or lived it out—or that it even be proved in the classroom.

Characteristics and Significance of Dewey's Writing

Several observations about Dewey's style of writing and argumentation are helpful in order to best understand his ideas. First, it has often been recognized and almost as often forgiven that Dewey's carelessness in syntax and logic frequently mars his philosophical discourse and frustrates the reader. He is also redundant, both within a given work and from one book or article to the next. It is possible that Dewey adopted this style for rhetorical purposes, employing repetition to hammer home his argument to as wide an audience as possible; the ideas and arguments that he most often repeats are usually his most important.

The vagueness that marks Dewey's most cherished concepts usually proves most frustrating to his readers. Alan Ryan kindly understates the problem, suggesting that Dewey's writing is "deliberately unstylish." Another of Dewey's intellectual biographers, Robert Westbrook, downplays Dewey's poor style, dryly commenting that "precision and clarity often escaped him." Supreme Court Justice Oliver Wendell Holmes called Dewey's writing "inarticulate," and William James said it was "damnable; you might even say God-damnable."[19] Political philosopher and journalist Hannah Arendt found Dewey's thought too divorced from real life, and she complained of the ambiguity of his thought: "What makes it so difficult to review this philosophy is that it is equally hard to agree or to disagree with it."[20] Dewey himself admitted late in life that he had "used language *ad hoc*."[21] Thomist philosopher Jacques Maritain not only notes the "ambiguities" in Dewey's writing, but also suggests "a disastrous confusion of ideas" therein.[22] Political scientist Leo R. Ward admits that John Dewey is "our most influential American philosopher of education." Ward explains, however, that it is hard to understand so much of Dewey's thought because "it is difficult to say for sure in what Dewey believed." Ward continues, "This confident man, exuding and inspiring confidence, may be seen as a man all his life in search of himself."[23]

Perhaps, though, it is this very vagueness and confusion that has made Dewey's work so resilient. The obscurity of his writing has conferred upon Dewey a kind of mystique that has allowed successive generations of philosophers and educators to argue, as Dewey himself did late in his career in *Experience and Education* (1938), that the misapplication of his educational philosophy is the consequence of a failure to grasp his ideas correctly. There is always, then, an opportunity for a revival of Dewey's thought, as yet one more scholar attempts to explain and accurately apply Dewey's *real* ideas. This is one reason why, despite withering attacks that might have consigned other thinkers to oblivion, Dewey is always able to rise again, Phoenix-like, as the hero of educational reform.[24] The irony is that educators often look to Dewey for solutions to problems that he himself created. Thus, a thorough airing and dissection of his thought is all the more imperative if we are to forestall the decline of American education before it has passed the point of recovery.

Some will undoubtedly protest that I have failed *to understand* Dewey, an objection that often serves as a talisman to ward off all criticism of his philosophy. Dewey, though, is not that difficult to understand if one is willing to accept the obvious—namely, that his arguments are ideologically charged and philosophically vague. Dewey subordinates his philosophy to his politics. I know this sounds harsh, but it is true, and it is the key to unlocking the purported difficulties of his thought.

What Dewey was not able to accomplish through the cogency of his arguments, he tried to supply by the sheer volume of his writing: his oeuvre has often overwhelmed both academic and lay readers by its bulk alone. In this book, I refer to many of Dewey's works, but I have placed special emphasis on the four works in which he presents his educational thought most directly: *Democracy and Education* (1916), perhaps his best-known work and the book in which he attempts to summarize his "entire philosophical position";[25] *Hu-*

man *Nature and Conduct: An Introduction to Social Psychology* (1922), which Dewey described as a study of "social conduct," but which is best characterized as a study of moral philosophy with important implications for moral education; *Schools of Tomorrow* (1915), which blends theory with a discussion of progressive educational practices; and *Experience and Education* (1938), an attempt to confront the many criticisms provoked by his lifelong effort at educational reconstruction.

At the time of its publication, one reviewer thought *Democracy and Education* (1916) as important as Plato's *Republic* and Rousseau's *Emile*. It has since been translated into a number of languages, including Arabic, Chinese, German, Italian, Japanese, Persian, Portuguese, Spanish, Swedish, and Turkish.[26] Its influence is difficult to overstate. William H. Kilpatrick "employed it as the bible of Columbia Teachers [College]," where he taught thousands of education majors.[27] It is tightly organized and succinctly argued, containing all of Dewey's important concepts. Many of these concepts, however, are discussed only superficially. For that reason, *Democracy and Education* may be Dewey's least objectionable work, since no subject is treated in great depth before another topic is introduced. Furthermore, all of these concepts are woven together in a philosophical system that appears at once coherent and plausible, so much so that it may seem difficult to identify a strategic point of criticism. Finally, Dewey's linkage of educational reform and democratic progress is ingenious and bestows a kind of universal appeal and philosophical orthodoxy on this work. The title itself reflects Dewey's grand theme that the future of American democracy is dependent on a revolution in American education, and that schools must therefore become the engines of democratic and social reform. *Democracy and Education*—or excerpts thereof—is the book most likely to be chosen in a school of education or department of political science as an introduction to Dewey's thought.

Human Nature and Conduct contains Dewey's most comprehensive criticism of traditional character development. *Human Nature and Conduct* is, also, in many ways, Dewey's most revealing
work. Since for Dewey "all morality is social," his inclusion of the
word "social" in the subtitle of this work is significant, in that it
reflects his opposition to any traditional notion of *individual* character: ethics for Dewey is exclusively a social matter, even though he
finds it useful to retain much of the classical vocabulary of moral
philosophy. *Human Nature and Conduct* began as a series of lectures
Dewey offered in the spring of 1918, lectures delivered, in part, to
suggest an alternative to the more individualistic theories of moral
behavior popular in his day, including those suggested by Freudian
psychoanalysis.[28] In this book he sought to articulate a psychology
suitable for democratic practice, one that would provide the theoretical foundation for progressive democratic change in the post–
World War I period. Dewey wished to demonstrate how the social
dynamics between the members of a participatory democracy might
take place, and how such dynamics could furnish the moral basis of
a democratic society. One sympathetic reviewer proclaimed, rightly,
that *Human Nature and Conduct* "dethrones all the idols of the
moralists."[29] Alan Ryan notes, "The politics of works like *Human
Nature and Conduct* never got in the way of their acceptance as texts,
partly because Dewey's politics were so much part of his philosophy
that readers had no sense that he was launching a political campaign."[30]

Taken with *Democracy and Education, Schools of Tomorrow*
(1915) elevated Dewey to the status of principal leader and spokesman for the progressive movement. (Dewey relied upon his dis-
ciple, W. H. Kilpatrick, to implement many of his ideas through
Teachers College, Columbia University, where Kilpatrick taught for
twenty-eight years.) Finally, late in his career, Dewey attempted a
kind of apologetic, *Experience and Education* (1925), as an effort to
confront the many criticisms provoked by his lifelong revolt against
conventional education. The longer one reads *Experience and Edu-*

cation, however, the more disturbed one becomes at this intemperate and disingenuous volume in which Dewey does little more than reiterate his leading ideas as he once again castigates traditional educational notions as harshly as ever.

Other important Dewey works, while not directly about education, nonetheless provide elucidation for the ideas in his explicitly educational texts. If *Democracy and Education* is Dewey's major work in education, some argue that *Experience and Nature* (1925) is of equal importance as a general philosophical work. The book was an attempt to satisfy critics who complained that Dewey's ideas were obscure and difficult to follow. If Dewey can be said to have a theory of metaphysics, it is his faith in experience. This metaphysics, moreover, is described as "naturalism," although the explanation thereof in some ways better indicates what Dewey does not believe rather than what he does believe. If there is meaning in life, Dewey argues, it is to be found fully in the material world and our experience thereof. Belief in the supernatural or any other search for transcendence is futile. To the extent Dewey has a system to interpret this metaphysics, it is his reliance upon the scientific method. This means that the only real guidance available to human beings is the observation of experience and the ongoing attempt to find and verify hypotheses to explain it. Hence, he explains in his preface that this book is about "empirical naturalism" or "naturalistic empiricism"—the reader may take his pick. Dewey's "naturalistic method," moreover, is a "winnowing fan" by which the "chaff" of life may be sifted from the wheat, the latter defined as consisting only of that which is scientifically verifiable (EE, ix–x; 1a).

The Quest for Certainty (1929) is a work of skepticism, despite Dewey's insistence that it is not. It is the product of a series of lectures in Edinburgh in the spring of 1929, lectures that were, by all accounts, enthusiastically received. The book has two theses. In the first, Dewey criticizes all previous philosophical and religious dogma as vain attempts to secure assurance about life and morals when such assurance is not possible. To allay his fears, for example, early man invented religion; later civilizations crafted philosophy for the same purpose. Secondly, recalling to mind the phrase associated with Kant, Dewey announces a kind of "Copernican revolution" or "Copernican reversal" whereby the scientific method becomes the sure guide to life.[31] The *Quest for Certainty* is also one of Dewey's books in which his attack on religion and tradition is especially salient.

The *Public and Its Problems* (1927) is the volume most concerned with political principles. In it Dewey explains that the failure of American democracy, as he perceives it, is found in the inadequacy of our understanding and experience of the "public." The concept of the "public," Dewey argues, should now replace that of the "individual," which he explains has been the traditional basis of liberal democracy. The emergence of the "public" depends upon greater communication, which will in turn facilitate a meaningful inquiry into how attention to the "public" might foster a more humane democratic experience. In other words, the precise meaning of the public, like so many of Dewey's ideas, awaits discovery through inquiry and experimentation; Dewey cannot at this time define it. The *Public and Its Problems* (1927) was motivated by social critic Walter Lippman's arguments doubting the ability of a democratic citizenry to engage fully in self-government.[32] Lyndon B. Johnson reportedly took the phrase "The Great Society" from this book to describe his ambitious social policy agenda.[33] Ironically, however, in *The Public and Its Problems*, Dewey argues that Americans must leave behind "The Great Society," the product of modern industrialization, in favor of "The Great Community." In that way, the "public" is recovered from the tangle of the impersonal machinery of contemporary life (PP, 126–27, 147, 157).

Dewey compiled *Reconstruction in Philosophy* (1920) from lectures delivered at Waseda University in Japan during his extended visit there and his subsequent visit to China. He later suggested that a more apt title might have been "Reconstruction *of* Philosophy" because the thesis of his book is his wholesale rejection of existing philosophic and religious movements in favor of his conception of naturalism. Although everything Dewey wrote revolved around education, Dewey sought a comprehensive philosophy under which all his intellectual interests might be subsumed. Late in his career he tackled the subject of art in *Art as Experience* (1934), arguing that the merit of art is in the experience of the beholder, not in its intrinsic genius or beauty. Dewey also sought, in the seventh chapter of *Reconstruction in Philosophy* and more fully in *Logic: The Theory of Inquiry* (1938), to redefine logic as mostly a quest guided by observation and hypothesis, thus demonstrating how wedded he was to the scientific method in every intellectual undertaking conceivable.

Jay Martin offers a tragicomic account of Dewey's endeavor, while in his nineties, to write a comprehensive text on philosophy. The anticipated title was *Naturalism* and Dewey expected it could be the summation of his life's work. But he lost the only copy of the manuscript in New York on a return to his Fifth Avenue apartment after a trip away: "My heavens, my brief case isn't here."[34]

After this introductory chapter, chapters 2 and 3 are a summary of the principal features of Dewey's educational thought. Chapter 4 is a kind of excursus in which I compare the educational thought of John Dewey with that of Thomas Jefferson, in particular, and, the American founding generation, in general. Dewey claimed to be the heir of Jefferson's democratic ideals, which Dewey hoped to promote through his own education philosophy. This, however, is a misleading if not disingenuous boast on Dewey's part, as this chapter demonstrates. Chapter 5, "A Useful Education," leaves a discussion of Dewey aside so as to draw upon other prominent educational philosophers to consider what makes for a truly profitable education, and whether a "useful" education must be opposed to tradition. Finally, chapter 6 offers concrete steps for overcoming the Dewey legacy.

Some will protest that any serious work on Dewey must take into account the vast amount of secondary literature in which several generations of academics have made their careers writing about Dewey—but more often writing about what the last person has written about Dewey. At some point, such activity reaches a point of diminishing return. With respect to Dewey, that point was undoubtedly passed decades ago. The French eighteenth-century essayist Montaigne anticipated the modern academic mimesis in which writers trade views on various subjects, and then trade views on their respective views until the original subject is all but forgotten, and perhaps badly understood. As Montaigne noted of the state of "serious" writing in his own day, "It is more of a business to interpret the interpretations than to interpret the texts." Montaigne likens such "scholarship" to the activity of Aesop's hungry dogs. The canines saw a corpse floating at a distance at sea but it was too far to retrieve by swimming. So, they set about "lapping up the water so as to dry out a path to it, and suffocated themselves."[35] With Montaigne's admonition in mind, I have tried not to write yet one more interpretation of Dewey's work. Such books comprise a vast body of water. This book, for the most part, is a simple exegesis of Dewey's writing, with commentary suggesting how his thought finds expression in contemporary American education. To adhere to that plan, the reader will find that I have quoted Dewey liberally so as best to illuminate his thought. "Give a man enough rope and he will hang himself," the proverb suggests.

Like the prodigal son, the educational establishment in this country has wandered from its inheritance. This inheritance comes from ancient Greece through the Judeo-Christian tradition and the best of Enlightenment thought, especially the ideas of the nation's founders. Perhaps the most significant development in our apostasy is the departure from common sense in favor of grand schemes of classroom experimentation. Consequently, too many students feed on the husks of pigs, a sorry meal that often leaves them intellectually, morally, and spiritually famished.

2

=

A New Way to Be Human

> How could one possibly agree with [Dewey's] philosophy, prid-
> ing itself on its closeness to reality and experience, which is
> actually so lost in abstract argument that . . . one feels . . .
> happily inside a paradise which rapidly turns out to be a fool's
> paradise?   — Hannah Arendt

DEWEY'S UNRELENTING ATTACK ON RELIGION and traditional
education is a conspicuous feature of his educational philosophy. It is
surprising, however, how easily Dewey has been forgiven for his
hostility to tradition, a prejudice that startles any open-minded reader.[1]
Dewey forthrightly maintains that a key obstacle to proper education
is traditional religion. Religion, he argues, "has lost itself in cults,
dogmas, and myths." It has become "perverted" and has generated "a
slavery of thought and sentiment." Like Nietzsche, Dewey believes that
conventional religion has created a "slave morality": Religion is "an
intolerant superiority on the part of the few and an intolerable burden
on the part of the many" (HNC, 330–31). In regard to the traditional
religious hope of an afterlife, and with reference to the notorious
statement generally attributed to Marx, Dewey asserts that "religion is
the opium of the people."[2]

Dewey makes little attempt to veil his hostility to Christianity in
particular. He writes, "For Christendom as a whole, morality has been

connected with supernatural commands, rewards and penalties."
He commends those who have "escaped this delusion" (HNC, 294;
RP, 120). Christianity is a "dying myth," nothing more than a "pic-
turesque" utopia or "irrelevant" dogma that contributes nothing to
"constructive action" (HNC, 297; EE, 221). Turning the Scripture verse
on its head, Dewey warns how easily one may be deceived *into* religious belief: "The path of truth is narrow and straitened" and "[i]t
is only too easy to wander beyond the course from this side to that."
Religion "has made morals fanatic or fantastic, sentimental or authoritative by severing them from actual facts and forces" (HNC,
296). Dewey reaffirmed his position on the occasion of his ninetieth
birthday, when he asserted that the "educational process is based
upon faith in human good sense and human good will"—but only
if individuals are "progressively liberated from bondage to prejudice
and ignorance," that is, orthodox faith.[3]

According to Dewey, religious moralists separate morals from
everyday life and encourage self-centeredness by focusing individuals on their own character instead of wider social concerns. Believers
are guilty of a kind of "spiritual egotism, . . . preoccupied with the
state of their character, concerned for the purity of their motives
and goodness of their souls" (HNC, 7). This preoccupation is nothing more than self-interested "conceit" and it is the "exaltation" of
this conceit that degenerates into self-absorption. This self-absorption produces "a corrosive inhumanity" that Dewey asserts is the
worst kind of selfishness. When this selfishness is religiously inspired
it produces individuals who are persistently preoccupied with another world, and this preoccupation breeds a "morbid discontent"
with contemporary life, ultimately degenerating into "a futile with-
drawal into an inner world" (HNC, 7). Given these views, it is no
surprise that Dewey signed the famous "Humanist Manifesto" in
1933, a secularist call to arms that emphatically rejects religious faith,
insisting that man face his difficulties and pursue his dreams "alone,"
without seeking consolation in, or assistance from, "supernaturalism."[4]

Dewey not only rejects conventional religion, he seeks to create a kind of alternative faith. In *Our Common Faith* (1934), he redefines the essence of religious experience as nothing more than a kind of shared democratic faith guided by science. He heralds the opportunity to free religion from supernaturalism because, in a modern democracy, "all the elements for a religious faith" are available instead in the "continuing life of this comprehensive community" that we call a democracy (OCF, 87, 85). Elsewhere, he makes nature into a kind of deity or else conflates nature with God. For example, he says, "Nature is both beneficent and truth its work; it retains all the properties of the Supreme Being."[5] At some point, after educational reforms have done their work, Dewey predicts that the "religious spirit will be revivified," although it is doubtful that what he means by "religion" would have much resemblance to any of the historical religions with which he was familiar (RP, 210).

To the extent American education has absorbed Dewey's enmity against religion, students and parents legitimately question whether their own values receive due respect in our liberal pluralistic society. Nowhere has genuine faith been more scorned, both by condescension and hostility, than in the halls of the educational establishment. As Gilbert Sewall, director of the American Textbook Council explains, "Tomorrow's curriculum is now developed in large part by educators trained in psychology, the human potential movement, and health education, many of whom have limited personal respect for and knowledge of venerable cultural traditions, especially religious ones."[6]

Some, however, argue that Dewey simply wanted students to become more reflective, to think for themselves. But however much they might wish that were true, that is not what he promoted. Although much of what Dewey said is vague, this much is clear: If a child clings to religion, tradition, or any other inherited values, he is not thinking "intelligently." Indeed, if a student were to claim to know what is "true," he might receive a low mark from Dewey because such a claim would be *ipso facto* proof positive that he is not "intelligent."

Human Nature Revised

James Madison writes in *Federalist* 51, "What is government itself but the greatest of all reflections on human nature?" Madison's famous rhetorical question might be paraphrased to apply to that most important of governmental activities, education by asking, "What is education itself but the greatest of all reflections on human nature?" Accordingly, to appreciate Dewey's radicalism one must understand his rejection of conventional notions of human nature in favor of his own innovations. These new conceptions, moreover, underlie all of his educational ideas and proposals and may go a long way toward explaining the contemporary decline in both academics and character education.

Dewey's idea of human nature is quite vague. One thing, however, is clear: for Dewey, human nature is not fixed; it can be changed and molded. Since human nature is not static, therefore, Dewey doggedly maintains an unflagging optimism in the possibility of progress. Dewey argues, moreover, that those very impulses of the student which traditional religion teaches us to restrain are the ones that educators should regard as their point of departure, instead of as demons to be exorcized. It is not clear what these impulses are which religion allegedly has induced us to suppress. For his part, Dewey insists that the traditional classroom has stifled the child's curiosity, creativity, and excitement for learning. Indeed, he seems to suggest that juvenile impulsivity itself must be liberated from misguided adult tutelage. Dewey argues time and again that the "impulses" as well as the interests of children should be the leading and organizing factors in the school day, replacing customary notions of discipline and preconceived courses of study.

Existing views of human nature, Dewey argues, serve chiefly

as pretexts for achieving social control. They are the tools by which rulers, political leaders, parents, and teachers have maintained their power over those that they govern, especially schoolchildren. This situation constitutes a misuse of schoolhouse authority as students have been the victims of social suppression just as surely as the citizens of an oppressive government are the victims of political tyranny. The traditional—but pernicious—definition of "good," Dewey alleges, is to do what you are told, nothing more. Dewey allows that although such classroom misgovernment may be well intentioned, it is still pedagogical abuse (HNC, 2–3).

Dewey's rejection of traditional views of human nature is critical to his purpose even though he admits that he has no real alternative by which to guide classroom activity. Rather, he proposes the development of hypotheses that may be tested in the classroom, and from that, he hopes useful, if tentative, conclusions might be drawn to guide further educational progress. Notwithstanding the risk of such experimentation, Dewey hopes this method will allow teachers and students alike to better understand what people are really like. Despite his professed scientific neutrality about the nature of man, there is no question that Dewey's belief in the goodness and pliability of human nature leans heavily toward that which one finds in the writing of Jean-Jacques Rousseau. Thus, for Dewey, the child needs little discipline or correction. Instead, the teacher's duty is to understand and follow the student's interest and "impulse." A child not yet discouraged by traditional education is still marked "by ardent curiosity, fertile imagination, and love of experimental inquiry."[7]

Dewey is careful to separate himself, at least rhetorically, from the Rousseauistic "romantic glorification of natural impulse as something superior to all moral claims" (HNC, 6). Such protestations, however, cannot obscure the fact that, on balance, Dewey's view of human nature is much closer to Rousseau's doctrine of natural innocence than he cares to admit, or perhaps than he even realizes.[8] Dewey's student, if properly managed, will spontaneously manifest a delight in learning. The typical strategy of rewarding students for success and punishing them for failure—the old "carrot-and-stick" approach—does not really encourage moral growth or learning. Indeed, once freed from such counterproductive supervision, the student learns automatically and autonomously.

With Dewey's approach to education, the pupil's mistakes no longer "assume undue importance or discourage him." The only student who will not benefit will be the "the really bad character." The "temptation to cheat" will all but disappear, since the "moral value of working for the sake of what is being done is certainly higher than that of working for rewards." In elementary and secondary school, at least, grading systems would be counterproductive: "Rewards and high marks are at best artificial aims to strive for; they accustom children to expect to get something besides the value of the product for work they do." Following Dewey's plan, "artificial inducements to work are no longer necessary" (ST, 297–99).

Dewey next announces a new morality that concentrates upon the "interaction" of the individual with his social world. This interaction he calls "habit," which is the exclusive possession of neither the individual nor his environment. In crafting this hypothesis, Dewey is giving an entirely new meaning to the word "habit," formerly associated with personal character traits. To be sure, he concedes, "The word habit may seem twisted somewhat from its customary use when employed as we have been using it" (HNC, 40).[9] Two observations of Dewey's position on this issue are pertinent. First, this conception of habit as the interaction of the individual and the social will always remain ambiguous, a flaw acknowledged by Dewey's supporters and critics alike. The second important point is that despite Dewey's attempt to steer a middle course between individual and social responsibility, with this redefinition of habit, the responsibility for individual misbehavior almost always falls on the shoulders of the group, rather than the individual.

Consequently, Dewey's new ethics introduces a serious accountability problem. To whom, or to what, is a student responsible for one's behavior? And how is educational progress to be measured? Dewey argues that only if an individual were totally "alone in the world" would his "habits . . . belong to him alone." In that instance, "responsibility and virtue would be his alone." But habits are a matter of "environing conditions," such as "a society or some specific group of fellow-men." Therefore, "[c]onduct is always shared. . . . It is not an ethical "ought" that conduct *should* be social. It *is* social, whether bad or good" (HNC, 16–17). So as not to leave his reader in any doubt, Dewey, by way of illustration, applies this principle to criminal justice, noting that, in his view, responsibility for crime is mistakenly ascribed to criminals, by which ascription "[s]ociety excuses itself" (HNC, 18). He argues, "Until we know the conditions which have helped form the characters we approve and disapprove, our efforts to create the one and do away with the other will be blind and halting." We cannot expect people to change their behavior until we fully understand the social dynamics in which they live (HNC, 19).

At War with Virtue

Dewey tends to ridicule the time-honored concepts of personal integrity, character, and "virtues," all of which he variously refers to as "magic" or "fatuity." Dewey asserts that in traditional character education, the pupil "is trained like an animal rather than educated like a human being" (DE, 13). Moral philosophers historically have taught that a "habit" is a fixed character trait: a person with a habit of loyalty, for example, is one on whom we can count "through thick and thin" because loyalty is a fixed part of his character. Against this view Dewey maintains that all of those traits that we typically think should be inculcated in children should no longer be the focus of moral education, for it is wrong to associate specific traits of character with an individual. He asserts that "[h]onesty,

chastity, malice, peevishness, courage, triviality, industry, irrespon-
sibility" are not the private possessions of a person but are instead
what he calls "working adaptations of personal capacities with
environing forces," for which no one seems to be accountable (HNC,
15–16).

Dewey also eliminates the "will" from any meaningful role in
moral development. This is no minor philosophical innovation; on
the contrary, the "will" has traditionally been identified as the faculty of moral choice. Indeed without the will, it is no longer meaningful to speak of moral *choice*, since it is one's will that does the
choosing. The problem is compounded given that there is, for Dewey,
no longer virtue or vice between which to choose. He explains that
although we have tended to "think of habits as means, waiting, like
tools in a box, to be used by conscious resolve," such a view is misguided because of its reliance upon the operation of the will (HNC,
27). At this point, Dewey's argument becomes confused because he
now offers the curious assertion that habit and will are, in fact, syn-
onymous. He writes, "Habit means . . . will" (HNC, 42).

We will see more fully in the next chapter that Dewey stresses
the importance of following the student's inclinations as a guide to
setting the curriculum. It is important at this point to note that a
child-led curriculum does not allow sufficient room for the development of the will. In his important but underappreciated response to
Dewey's educational philosophy, Jamie Castiello explains that such
pedagogy, guided chiefly by a child's interests, produces students lack-
ing in reason and character, too often led by nothing more than their
whim. The "appeal to reason is disappearing from many classrooms,"
he explains: "[C]hildren are only to be taught art when they spontaneously look at a picture and feel an emotional interest in it; in other
words when they 'feel like it.' Such an education does away with 'willing,' which can indeed be present even when 'One does not feel like
it.'" Castiello concludes, "It is well to remember that in order to con-
quer life man must start by conquering himself."[10]

As every parent knows, something has gone dreadfully wrong with classroom behavior. Political philosopher (and parent) J. Martin Rochester notes of education today, "It is hard to say which is declining faster, academic standards or ethical standards."[11] Sociologist James Davison Hunter observes that traditional moral education has suffered the onslaught of a militant campaign bent on its eradication, noting, that "character in America has not died a natural death. There has been an ironic and unintended complicity among the very people who have taken on the task of being its guardians and promoters."[12] Thus, despite a growing consensus that character must once again be taught in schools, educators struggle more than one might expect with such a straightforward task. Why? The answer lies, in large measure, in the progressive philosophy that still undermines these efforts. That philosophy largely comes from John Dewey and his "devaluation of character education," Hunter concludes. One notable instance is "Values Clarification," the popular substitute for character education in the 1970s, which was inspired by Dewey's writing.[13]

Dewey's attack on the pedagogical goal of personal character is also evident in the conspicuous preoccupation among professional educators with "self-esteem." While all would agree that a healthy self-image is necessary for an individual's well being, contemporary educators often ignore the truth that self-esteem is built upon achievement. Advocates of progressive education argue that the teacher can artificially construct a student's self-esteem with praise in the absence of success—or sometimes even effort—through programs such as "I Like Me." Proponents of these kinds of programs are floundering in the confusion of the Deweyan tradition. Denied virtue as the basis upon which student success is built, educators must innovate with short cuts that attempt the isolated promotion of psychological well-being. It also should come as no surprise that teachers regularly complain that students don't make "good choices," given the depreciation of the student's means of choosing, the human will.

Despite Dewey's influence, a revival of the concept of personal virtue has emerged both in popular culture and in classrooms, given the general deterioration of conduct and order among many young people. This revival comes in the shape of various kinds of school and civic "character" programs. Most startling about this "rediscovery of virtue," however, is that the pursuit of personal character could have been abandoned in the first place.

Lab Rats or Students?

Dewey stresses that all doctrines, whether philosophical or religious, are no more than "hypotheses" until they are tested and verified. This view forms the thrust of all of his work, but it is made most explicit in *Quest for Certainty* (1929), in which he longs for a time when "the experimental theory" might form the core "of every person's working attitude toward life" (QC, 271, 277). What Dewey fails to acknowledge—or perhaps grasp—is that not all phenomena can be "tested" by empirical observation and verification. Perhaps, though, he simply finds it convenient to use the prestige accorded the scientific method to discredit that which he already disbelieves, namely "the truth of creeds, religious, moral and political." Such beliefs, with their attendant "intolerance and fanaticism," mislead us into supposing that there exist "inherent truth and authority."[14]

Whatever may be his motivation, Dewey believes that the scientific method of observation, hypothesis, and experimentation must now be the intellectual engine of the schoolhouse. Dewey refers to scientific methodology as "intelligence," which he designates as the proper *modus operandi* of the school once traditional pedagogy is set aside (DE, 228). The scientific method will enable educators to relinquish "the crutch of dogma, of beliefs fixed by authority" (DE, 339). Dewey argues that if traditionally minded pedagogues resist his project of schoolhouse experimentation, the curriculum will consist of nothing more than a study of "the classics, of languages no longer spoken" (DE, 229). Such empiricism, moreover, lies at the heart of the "critical thinking" Dewey has in mind for his students. It is this scientistic dogma that he insists they must acquire and practice.

Here we begin to see that Dewey's student is not nearly so free to decide for himself what is academically worthwhile as Dewey suggests, for hovering above all such judgments is Dewey's own criterion of "utility." If, for example, poetry cannot be made into "a resource in the business of life," it is "artificial poetry," or in other words, not an authentic object of study. Furthermore, those value judgments that the student does undertake are subject to constant reevaluation by the teacher to ensure their instrumental value and to weed out the inevitable but dangerous accumulation of purely traditional material, or, as Dewey puts it, "inherited matter." Such evaluation is no doubt a difficult task. But one measure of instrumental value is the student's response: "When pupils are genuinely concerned in learning Latin, that is of itself proof that it possesses value." What students like is what is valuable and useful (DE, 231–42).

Dewey argues, moreover, that only the full integration of the scientific method into education can create a democratic classroom and prepare students to resolve the intractable social problems that await them. For Dewey, "every step forward" in the social sciences will depend upon "the method of collected data, forming hypotheses, and testing them in action." There is no other wisdom for guiding human affairs (DE, 285). It only remains, he asserts, to apply scientific thinking to such especially "perplexing problems as insanity, intemperance, poverty, public sanitation, city planning, [and] the conservation of natural resources" (DE, 285). Although Dewey in later years would try to distance himself from irresponsible if not scandalous progressive experimentation, he should not have been surprised that his authority would be cited to justify both the denigration of textbook learning and also the outright exclusion of textbooks from the classroom in favor of unpredictable and unaccountable classroom wandering. The price of such experimentation, more-over, is that, the "subjects" of the experiment—the pupils—must suffer the experimenter's mistakes. When dealing with *human* sub-jects such a cost cannot be justified.

As we noted above, Dewey is unable to offer a better explana-tion of human nature than that provided in the classical and Chris-tian intellectual traditions. Rather, his ambition is to encourage ex-perimentation in the hope of *discovering* such an explanation, since, in his view, our present "science" of human nature is "elementary" and does not promote well-being. This rather naïve faith in the abil-ity of science to provide comprehensive answers to all questions was, of course, not unusual in the first half of the twentieth century. But although intellectual enthusiasm for this sort of raw scientism has waned, Dewey's zeal for a scientific approach to education has left an indelible mark on both educational theory and practice.

Dewey complains that without scientific observation and analysis we can know nothing reliable about moral behavior. If we are to get anywhere, science must replace religious or philosophical guidance. He thus deprives the educator of the traditional task of moral formation but offers nothing to replace it other than an am-biguous hypothesis to be explored. The classroom will become the laboratory wherein morality is investigated as one might pursue ex-periments in electricity, pathology, or physics. Indeed, at times Dewey argues that morality *is* experimentation, not the object to be discov-ered by experimentation. Moral deliberation, he notes, proceeds by experimentation, and moral choice is no more than "simply hitting in imagination upon an object" (HNC, 190, 193).

A recent column in *Newsweek* by a retired school teacher mer-its extended quotation because it illustrates the consequence of Dewey's experimentalism in schools today. The author expresses the frustration of one who has seen the classroom made the occasion for careless experimentation.

There has never been an innovation or reform that has
helped children learn any better, faster or easier than they
did prior to the 20th century. I believe a case could be made
that real learning was better served then than now. . . . What
baffles me is not that educators implement new policies
intended to help kids perform better, it's that they don't
learn from others' mistakes. . . . The old way is the best way.
. . . Reform movements like new math and whole language
have left millions of damaged kids in their wake. We've
wasted billions of taxpayer dollars and forced our teachers
to spend countless hours in workshops learning to implement the latest fads. Every minute teachers have spent on
misguided educational strategies (like building kids' self-
esteem, by acting as "facilitators" who oversee group projects)
is time they could have been teaching academics. . . . We
should stop using students as lab rats and return to a more
traditional method of teaching.[15]

To be sure, Dewey's educational ideas are more abstract than
the ideals he so emphatically condemns and rejects. Dewey's experimentation means that unproven theory becomes the subject matter
of the classroom. This has led to a long train of untested practices
introduced to students, often with worse results than the previous
unproven theory. These ideas are sometimes more supportive of the
professional careers of school administrators and the tenure of university faculty than they are beneficial to students. Even though
Dewey regularly condemned traditional education because of its
tolerance of "ideals," he has helped spawn an academic way of life in
schools that is far more intangible, and is often detached from the
real business of learning. Dewey complains in *Experience and Nature* (1925) that traditional ideas and schooling are inspired by "private fantasy" or "Olympian aloofness"; yet, this book may be the
most frustratingly abstract of all his texts. Dewey argues therein that
anything but his faithless materialistic system of experimentation
and verification is "aloof" and "abstract." He further insists that

education must be "concrete" and it must lead back to "ordinary life-experiences." Yet, he justifies burdening school systems with obscure pedagogical theories, predicated on wishful views of human nature, and conceived in the artificial environment of "laboratory schools" (EN, 436, 6, 7, 39).

Dewey's enthusiasm for turning the classroom into the testing ground for experimentation has provided the justification for doing so ever since. Making education the opportunity for pursuing theoretical novelty has created an ever-widening chasm between theory and practice so that contemporary educational theories are too often irrelevant to real learning.

The most astonishing symbol of education's surrealistic separation between theory and practice is this: although he has told millions how to teach elementary and secondary students, John Dewey himself was a poor teacher. He had trouble maintaining discipline in both the secondary teaching posts he occupied, and when he left the latter in Charlotte, Vermont, "the townspeople . . . were glad to see him depart."[16]

Classroom Nihilism

For all of his talk of creativity, progress, and growth, there is a destructive impulse in Dewey's educational philosophy. Alan Ryan admits that Dewey's ideas were not only "original" but "reckless."[17] The promise of Dewey's radical progressive education has failed to materialize. Entire school systems have abandoned proven methods of education in pursuance of Dewey's educational proposals. As Dewey himself states, fundamental discoveries "always entail the destruction or disintegration of old knowledge *before the new can be created*" (RP, xvi).[18] Elsewhere, he concedes that his "naturalistic method . . . destroys many things once cherished" (EE, ix–x). Yet his experimental method proves incapable of supplying an adequate substitute for that which it destroyed.

Indeed, reflections of Nietzschean nihilism are not hard to find in Dewey's thought.[19] We noted earlier in the chapter Dewey's use of Nietzsche's characterization of Christianity as a "slave morality," one in which one group is subjugated by another through religious doctrine. Dewey also suggests that the moral boundaries of "good and evil" are invalid in light of modern science, echoing Nietzsche's thesis in *Beyond Good and Evil*.[20] Dewey also echoes Nietzsche's assertion that the basis of morality is the "will to power" of the most advanced and creative members of society, and Dewey introduces this idea into the classroom.

More precisely, Dewey's idea of "impulse" leads in a troubling direction. At times, impulse involves passion or desire, but at other times it takes on a more disquieting character, as when Dewey condemns both conventional pedagogy and Christianity for suppressing impulse, which for him is tantamount to suppressing "selfhood." He advocates instead a new classroom ethic that allows for the "release" of impulses so that they might be "intelligently" employed. He argues, "If we can remove artificial labels and means of control from human nature then each impulse or habit is thus a will to its *own* power" (HNC, 137–40). Education cannot progress if impulses are "snubbed" or "sublimated." These impulses are so primeval that "frustration dams activity up, and intensifies it," and engenders a "longing for satisfaction at any cost." Ultimately, "the will to power bursts into flower" (HNC, 141). The result, more often than not, is pathological: "Explosive irritations, naggings, the obstinacy of weak persons, dreams of grandeur, the violence of those usually submissive are the ordinary marks of a will to power" (HNC, 142).

We all possess this "will to power," but, Dewey explains, it is generally restricted by social forms and repressive school practices in all but the most aggressive personalities, such as a "Napoleon" (HNC, 142).[21] Dewey further explains that individual creativity is a benefit of released impulse, and that his new classroom ethic will set educators "upon a course of social invention and experimental engineering."

Dewey then identifies the uninhibited emergence of impulse—
a primeval force not unlike Nietzsche's will to power that demands
creative expression—as that which defines individuality and potentially drives educational and social change. If the educator denies
the opportunity for its expression, it is likely to turn aggressive and
violent. In that case, culpability for such behavior would no doubt
rest with the school and educator, not the pupil. Indeed, a recent
article in a leading educational journal couples Dewey and the idea
of nihilism to call for "the reawakening of intensity of impulse" in
education. More generally, an increasingly popular theme in educational research today, evident in the leading educational academic
journals, is the application of Nietzsche's thought to the classroom.[22]
It is no wonder that traditional pedagogical discipline and restraints
must be eradicated. As Nietzsche himself explains, creators must
also be destroyers.[23]

The destructive tone of Dewey's philosophy sometimes appears in the form of an imbalanced and misguided obsession with
student creativity. Indeed, one popular expression of progressivism
in educational philosophy is "constructivism," a classroom approach
in which pupils are coached to "create their own meaning."
Constructivism, though, might better be called "destructivism/
constructivism" since "old realities" must give way if "new realities"
have room to appear. Educational nihilism also appears as "values
clarification" in which students may be taught to set aside tradition
and construct their own ethical framework."[24] Underlying such "innovative" pedagogy one often finds an unnecessary and irrational
hostility to traditional pedagogy. For that reason, at a great sacrifice
of resources, more and more families flee to private schools or stay
at home for education, settings where they will not have to battle
opposition to their ethnic, religious, or philosophical ideals.

As moral education grows less and less committed to propa-
gating some objective moral content, and as the authority that would
reinforce that content weakens, the clarity of a distinction between

some notion of good and evil necessarily fades. In both theory and practice, the ancient boundary markers have withered away. Hunter suggests that Dewey "was not troubled" by the erosion of the basic philosophical and theological distinctions of good and evil. Indeed, Hunter suggests that a commitment to objective truth is the linchpin that determines the success of moral education, arguing that absent such a commitment, all reform will be inadequate.[25] Not only is this nihilistic impulse evident in the destructive effect of contemporary educational ideas, it also surfaces in the harsh Nietzschean "will to power" that defines the political behavior of so many educational theorists, bureaucrats, legislators, and practitioners.

As noted previously, throughout his writing Dewey depreciates the use of books in the classroom, though this denigration may be explicit or implicit. The authority the curriculum once held has been undermined in the quest of a new progressive pedagogy. Worse still, we have now reached a point where many argue against the *possibility* of any academic canon at all. This is where Dewey's nihilism has taken us.

3

=

Dewey's Revolt

The effect of Dewey's philosophy on the design of curricular
systems was devastating.   — Richard Hofstadter

PROGRESSIVE EDUCATION HAS BECOME FAMOUS—or notori-
ous—for insisting that learning take place by *doing*. This means that
whether the subject is history, arithmetic, literature, or science, if it
cannot be learned through an activity its value is suspect. For this
reason, Dewey regularly denigrates "formal education," "mere bookishness," and "what is popularly termed the academic." Values that adults
typically "impose" upon students include, he explains, reverence for
academic subjects like the "classics of literature, painting, music."
Dewey argues that if these values and subjects are taught—rather than
experienced—they "will be *merely* symbolic."[1] Therefore, all curricula
and methods are subject to constant inspection if not revision to see if
they are worthwhile. Dewey is averse to the idea that anything might be
transmitted to students from the legacy of previous generations that
students do not experience themselves. Despite his celebrated pragmatism, he admits the obvious inefficiency inherent in the requirement
that students discover everything anew (DE, 234–35, 241).

Dewey also eschews the traditional categorization of subject material into, for example, sciences, literature, history, and math. The con-

ventional division of courses, he argues, is a historical artifact for which there is no intrinsic or instrumental justification. While many educators today recognize that interdisciplinary study may at times be appropriate, Dewey would discard all categorical designations so that learning might occur in a spontaneous fashion as each child is guided by his own interest and impulse. In taking such a position, Dewey must accept the considerable *impracticality* of abandoning all established means of organization in favor of the unknown.

For Dewey, there is no important distinction between education for leisure and education for work. Indeed, the liberal arts by definition mean subject material that is "free" or "liberated" from the demand for immediate relevance, but the idea of a "liberal education" finds no home with Dewey. He dismisses traditional liberal studies as "uselessness." Although Dewey agrees that there is a difference between "living" and "living worthily," he insists that such a life is not found by arbitrarily denoting some subjects as suitable for liberal studies and some as suitable for practical training. Ironically, Dewey would rid the school of liberal—or "free"—learning in the interest of *liberating* the student. Dewey's freedom will entail, he explains, "freedom from authority, freedom from the curriculum, [and] freedom from convention." As with some other progressive reformers, Dewey even argues that to require students to sit still may violate their liberty and frustrate their learning (DE, 257, 301, 305).

To be sure, Dewey is consistently anti-authoritarian, whether the source of authority be tradition, religion, or academic disciplines (DE, 246–47). He finds it "both astonishing and depressing that so much of the energy of mankind has gone into fighting for . . . the truth of creeds, religious, moral and political" with the "intolerance and fanaticism" that attend "beliefs and judgments" (QC, 277). Dewey offers a harsh choice to his readers: either follow his lead or else choose "a reactionary return to the educational traditions of the past" (HWT, 169).

By attending to the child's "interest," Dewey says that teachers can avoid earlier ways of learning that hamper good progressive
education (DE, 130). The problem with traditional "subject matter,"
Dewey alleges, is that it is not unique for every student; it is "indifferent" to their distinct personalities. If subject matter is not tai-
lored to the individual student, the student must waste "effort to
bring the mind to bear upon it." This would require "discipline of
the will," which, as we have seen, is, for Dewey, an unprofitable
exercise (DE, 133). He complains that a "peculiar artificiality attaches
to much of what is learned in schools" because formal learning "does
not possess for [students] the kind of reality which the subject matter of their vital experiences possesses." Even in matters of aesthetics, Dewey prohibits the teacher from recommending particular
works of art as having intrinsic worth. Avoiding such aesthetic judgments will aid in erasing the "division between laboring classes and
leisure classes" that the appreciation of the fine arts may foster (DE,
136).

But this promise of classroom liberty puts Dewey in a difficult position, because he has a particular agenda to which students
must subscribe if he is to shape them into change agents for the
common good. In order for the school to operate as he thinks it
should, Dewey recommends "conjoint activities" that allow the child
only to assist in organizing his own education. If children could
express themselves "articulately and sincerely," Dewey notes, "they
would tell a different tale," by which he means they would craft a
more worthwhile curriculum for themselves. Since they cannot express themselves, Dewey speaks for them (DE, 40). Dewey's defenders are correct when they protest that he did not advocate a classroom controlled by nothing more than a child's caprice—as did
some other progressive educationists. Rather, in Dewey's classroom,
the students' interests are channeled into politically and socially correct attitudes and activities.

Socialization, Not Education

Dewey argues that the educational experience should be, as much as possible, a microcosm of social life. If the schoolhouse is society on a small scale, then the socialization, not the mere education, of the pupil becomes the primary task of the educator. Education is no longer simply academic or even moral—it is the first step of an experiment in social change. In making a social revolution the purpose of education, Dewey begins to erase the boundaries that make school a unique institution. By merging school and society, Dewey believes, the school can be saved from irrelevant book learning and reconstructed so as both to resemble and produce a better society. Admittedly, the school may become distracted from its traditional responsibility of academic training, but such a risk does not deter Dewey. To the contrary, he seems eager to see schools turn away from "formal instruction" that "easily becomes remote and dead, abstract and bookish" (DE, 8).

Dewey admits that if socialization is the new objective of education, academics may suffer. He explains, "In achieving this goal . . . we must leave behind an 'unduly scholastic' and 'formal notion' of education" (DE, 4). To be sure, Dewey condemns the "usual isolated text-book study method." In his criticism of the "accumulation of facts presented in books," he decries the overemphasis allegedly placed upon the child's memory by means of rewards and punishments. In such an environment, Dewey writes, "The virtues that the good scholar will cultivate are the colorless, negative virtues of obedience, docility, and submission. By putting himself in an attitude of complete passivity he is more nearly able to give back just what he heard from the teacher or read in the book" (ST, 297).

Dewey explains that the teacher should furnish an "environment" rather than particular subject matter. This approach saves the pupil from becoming victim to "the formulated, the crystallized, and systematized subject matter of the adult." But what subject matter is Dewey criticizing? He answers, rather sweepingly, that it is "the material as found in books and in works of art, etc." Realizing that the student cannot learn in a vacuum, Dewey knows that some amount of authoritative subject matter may inadvertently filter into the student's experience despite the educator's best efforts to prevent it. In that case, the learning material must be scrutinized for its instrumental value to see if it has any immediate usefulness, since all subject matter is "tentative and provisional until its worth is tested experimentally" (DE, 189).

Dewey argues that just as gardening can be used as an informal environment to teach botany and chemistry, so also all meaningful subject matter can be taught through informal "hands-on" activity (DE, 182–83, 189, 194, 200). This means, for instance, that history is appropriate only insofar as it can be made immediately relevant to the present, after which it will be useful to cultivate "a socialized intelligence." Only in this way does the study of history have "moral significance." For Dewey, the idea that historical narratives might be used didactically to teach "moral lessons on this virtue or that vice" is a practice that belongs to an earlier age. Such an approach to history has no value and does no more than produce "a temporary emotional glow." Although it may not be Dewey's intention to depreciate historical study completely, he puts such restraints upon how it is to be undertaken that meaningful study becomes difficult.

An appreciation of Dewey's use of education as the vehicle of social change helps us to understand the 1980s idea of "Outcomes Based Education" (OBE). OBE was attractive upon introduction and generated considerable excitement in the educational establishment. It quickly became evident, however, that it often was an opportunity for politicization rather than a tool to ensure basic competencies in core subjects. More generally, educators today sometimes find that their well-intentioned reforms provoke a political firestorm because the public in general, and parents in particular, may discern political ambitions behind otherwise innocuous new techniques.

This politicization of education has colored even the writing of textbooks. In her troubling but revealing book, *The Language Police*, educational historian Dianne Ravitch describes the current process by which textbooks are chosen and rejected on the basis of narrow ideological prejudices. Textbooks are censored by "bias and sensitivity" committees to ensure they present proper attitudes toward race, gender, and Western culture. Literature anthologies are arranged so that the authors chosen provide proper representation to minority groups; the actual quality of the literature is a distant secondary consideration. Texts are overburdened with the social agenda of the day, while material deemed potentially "offensive" is systematically deleted. The consequence is biased, dull books.[2] This is America's inheritance from John Dewey. As distressing as programs such as OBE may be, and as disconcerting as textbook politics have become, one must understand that the use of the school to propagate a political program is an unfortunate legacy of Dewey's educational philosophy—which easily justifies such mischief.

Play and the Curriculum

In the interest of "testing" classroom material, Dewey attempts to erase the line distinguishing work and play. Dewey argues that play is often a more conducive environment to learning than work, because "experience has shown that when children have a chance at physical activities which bring their natural impulses into play, going to school is a joy, management is less of a burden, and learning is easier" (DE, 194). In *Schools of Tomorrow*, Dewey's discussion of "play" is especially revealing—and disturbing. The task of the educator, he explains, is to draw the "instinctive qualities" out of the child as unobtrusively as possible so that they are untainted by adult provincialism. Play activity is the best strategy for doing so, he explains. Predictably, however, Dewey places important qualifications on play. He notes that the "educational value" of play is that it "teaches the children about the world in which they live." The nature of play, he explains, is that it is "imitative." But there is a problem. Children may engage in play that is not supportive of Dewey's aspirations for social change. That is, they may imitate the wrong thing, namely the lives of their parents.

Indeed, Dewey's ambitious plans for the socialization of children are perhaps most remarkable in the absence of virtually any major role for the family. He asserts in *Democracy and Education* that since children are born ignorant of "the aims and habits of the social group . . . education, and education alone spans the gap." The role of families is essentially ignored in that influential book. In *Schools of Tomorrow* he implies that the home, more often than not, is an obstacle to proper socialization. Dewey warns that without proper supervision, the play of a child may constitute "a strong influence against change" if the child's play is merely "a replica of the life of his parents." For example, when they "play house, children are just as apt to copy the coarseness, blunders, and prejudices of their elders as the things which are best" (ST, 108, 3, 109).

For this reason, Dewey notes with approval what was transpiring in some of the progressive kindergartens of his day. These schools were providing directed play "for the educational value of the activities it involves, and for giving the children the right sort of ideals and ideas about every day life" (ST, 109). Many of these "ideals and ideas" were necessarily contrary to what children learn at home. Dewey hopes that children will take what they have learned and use it to reform the presumed deficiencies in their own families. Through properly guided play, children "will forget to imitate the loud and coarse things they see at home" (ST, 109–10). Conventional ideas regarding gender roles may be among the first misconceptions to fall, since the separate interests of boys and girls are socially conditioned, not natural.

Boys and girls alike take the same interest in all these occupations, whether they are sewing and playing with dolls, or
marble making and carpentry. The idea that certain games
and occupations are for boys and others for girls is a purely
artificial one that has developed as a reflection of the conditions existing in adult life. It does not occur to a boy that
dolls are not just as fascinating and legitimate a plaything
for him as for his sister, until some one puts the idea into
his head (ST, 115).

In this context, Dewey also notes the value of a kind of "practical civics," especially where immigrant families are concerned. He
hopes that schoolchildren will carry out measurements of their home
environment that their teachers can then keep on file. In so doing, it
will be "a simple matter" to determine whether families "are living
under proper moral and hygienic conditions" (ST, 201). Here we see
Dewey's reluctance to recognize a legitimately private domain. In
The Public and Its Problems, for example, he denies that, as an institution, the family has any inherent "sanctity." Dewey compares the
family to a labor union, to a business corporation, even to the state
itself, asserting that the worth of each is to be judged solely by its
"consequences" (PP, 74).

In this light, we should note that President Clinton initiated
his "Goals 2000: Educate America Act" in 1997 in order to monitor
states' progress in meeting objectives toward eight separate goals.
The goals include "School Completion," "Student Achievement and
Lifelong Learning" and "Safe, Disciplined, and Alcohol-and Drug-
Free Schools." "Parental Participation" is relegated to eighth place.
Curriculum standards were established for each subject area, incit-
ing widespread controversy because of their perceived bias.[3]

Truly academic study is conspicuously and consistently omit-
ted from Dewey's curriculum because it does not replicate any typical community activity. Neither can it demonstrate an immediate
social benefit to students or their neighborhoods. For Dewey, then,

civic education might be better called "socializing education." This more "enlarged use of the school plant" and expanded conception of the role of the school will produce what Dewey calls "a more intelligent public spirit" (ST, 228). Schools so animated are better equipped to encourage social and cultural change and less prone to the inertia produced by "tradition and custom" (ST, 229). Thus, the "Goals 2000" initiative was introduced by the Department of Education as "the best change agent we can have."[4]

The slave-turned-statesman Frederick Douglass writes that, prior to his emergence as a public figure, he memorized many speeches from the classic anthology, *The Columbian Orator*, as a means of developing his formidable rhetorical skills. These skills, together with his character, were instrumental in Douglass's role as an antislavery leader, both in America and abroad.[5] But Dewey seems to imply that such an "uncreative" activity as memorizing someone else's speeches would jeopardize a student's freedom and creative development. Indeed, rote memorization of *anything* is discouraged, for to do so would implicitly acknowledge that a body of information is authoritarian enough to warrant committing it to memory.

Education through Industry

Dewey envisions an education that is more vocational than academic in nature. This shift of focus is necessary, he argues, in order to place students in an "active" rather than passive learning posture in which information is "imparted by textbook and teacher" (ST, 238). To be sure, Dewey offers an unsettling commentary about the use of books in education. He says that in an earlier educational era the school needed to supply books to students because books were otherwise unavailable. They were often the only way in which a student might access the "great world beyond the village surroundings" (ST, 240). "But conditions change," Dewey insists, as "libraries abound, books are many and cheap, magazines and newspapers are everywhere" (ST,

242). For that reason, "the schools do not any longer bear the peculiar relation to books and book knowledge which they once did" (ST, 242). Although schools should encourage habits of reading, Dewey argues that "it is no longer necessary or desirable that the schools should devote themselves so exclusively to this phase of instruction" (ST, 243). The more important question for Dewey concerns the social and community uses to which students will employ what they have gained from their reading; he does not wish them "to waste themselves upon the trash which is so abundantly provided" in the classroom (ST, 244). Dewey eschews a "liberal and cultural" education because it lacks, in his judgment, a clear, immediate, and sure capacity for social change. Dewey also alleges that such an education perpetuates an ossified and unjust social structure. He stresses instead a general education that is highly vocational and from which "bookishness" has been purged.[6]

Dewey complains that it is "absolutely impossible" to culti-vate habits of social change "when schools devote themselves to the formal sides of language." In other words, Dewey recognizes that schools may not have sufficient time to teach students to read while also training them to change the world. Reading, then, must be deemphasized though he maintains that highly motivated social re-formers eventually will be stimulated to read anyway in order to investigate those things relevant to their activity (ST, 245). As soon as a student acquires a "lovely sense of the interest of social affairs" he will spontaneously turn to the books that support his interest (ST, 245). The time for an education organized around books, how-ever, is past. For Dewey, it is "fairly criminal" if students are taught skills but not induced to put those skills to prompt social use.

Dewey's motives for vocational education, or what he calls "education through industry," include, first of all, providing stu-dents with practical hands-on knowledge (ST, 265–66, 268), though not in the sense of what we would consider a "trade" education (ST, 309). For although he wants to give students "skills," Dewey is not interested in taking that training to the point of teaching a useful trade. To do so would distract from his larger social purpose. In addition, Dewey hopes that education through industry will erase social class distinctions heretofore associated with the line between academic and vocational training. To the extent that vocational tracks exist at progressive schools, he insists that they be put on an equal level with academic studies (ST, 262). Education through industry, Dewey argues, puts students into the active mode necessary for the challenges they will confront. Such a use of industrial education is important in making "the abuses and failures of democracy . . . disappear" (ST, 304).

Just as school should not be academic, then, neither should it be truly vocational. Dewey accordingly warns against a too closely defined vocational education program (DE, 310). He stipulates that vocational education be "indirect" rather than "direct," so that, as always, "the needs and interests of the pupil" are given free play. With such an approach, "vocational guidance" will not lead to a "definitive, irretrievable, and complete choice" that is likely to be "rigid, hampering further growth" (DE, 311). Although given the opportunity the vocational student might learn to be a good carpenter, he will not acquire the "freedom of thought" necessary to be a proper social reformer.

It appears that Dewey has been granted his wish as American schools, in general, are neither rigorously academic nor authentically vocational. Not only are American students deficient academically, they have little opportunity for meaningful vocational education. Though they may spend time with a meaningful craftsmanship project, authentic vocational training is often hard to find. Indeed, American education, at times, seems to eschew ideals both of academic excellence and also of vocational aptitude.

The National Endowment for the Arts' distressing study, "Reading at Risk," moreover, explains that American youth are rapidly losing an interest in, and the practice of, meaningful reading. It also further explains that it is precisely those who read the most books, and the most serious books, who are the most likely to be civically engaged. The authors report, "Literary reading strongly correlates to other forms of active civic participation. Literary readers are more likely than non-literary readers to perform volunteer and charity work, visit art museums, attend performing arts events, and attend sporting events."[7] The report suggests that, ironically, an education based on "activity" and directed toward social reform is far *less* likely to inspire needful social change than the "isolated" and "bookish" education that Dewey decries.

Ambiguous "Intelligence"

Dewey insists that what he calls "intelligence"—as opposed to custom, tradition, authority, or dogma—should guide moral deliberation and progress. "Intelligence," however, is another ambiguous term in Dewey's work even though this is one of his most important concepts. Dewey devotes considerable time to attacking what intelligence must replace, but comparatively little space in explaining what "intelligence" means (HNC, 184–85; EE, 436–37). It seems clear enough, however, that intelligence in some way must replace the faculty of reason, or at least that reason must be reworked into something called intelligence (RP, x, 96). Dewey's conception of intelligence also involves the use of the scientific method and that which is to be attained by the scientific method. At times, intelligence acquires an almost mystical dimension. "'It thinks' is a truer psychological statement than 'I think,'" explains Dewey. He further argues that although we cannot depend upon a rational universe, intelligence takes advantage of circumstances so as to win whatever fortune may yield. "Luck," Dewey argues, "has a way of favoring the intelligent and showing its back to the stupid" (HNC, 314, 305).

Dewey insists that intelligence must replace traditional morals and ideals. Intelligence, in turn, should produce "growth." But what is growth? Dewey can only answer tautologically: growth is that which is guided by intelligence. Progress is interestingly but unhelpfully described as "present reconstruction adding fullness and distinctness of meaning," while "retrogression is a present slipping away of significance, determinations, grasp" (HNC, 281). But to what does progress lead except to more progress? Dewey offers a superficially appealing but odd analogy: "If it is better to travel than to arrive, it is because traveling is a constant arriving, while arrival that precludes further traveling is most easily attained by going to sleep or dying" (HNC, 282; RP, 96–97).

Toward the end of his career, Dewey could provide no better explanation of "growth" than that it is "good," and when properly directed, encourages further growth. The only criteria for judging growth, he persists, is more growth. He writes, "The essential point is that the purpose grow and take shape through the process of social intelligence" (EE, 72). Then he asks, "Does this form of growth create conditions for further growth?" (EE, 36). His disappointing answer, even late in his career, is: "I shall leave you to answer these questions" (EE, 36).

Here as elsewhere, it must be said that Dewey leaves the student, parent, and educator perplexed. Each of the explanations given in his long train of clarifications is less understandable and more frustrating than the previous one. The consequence of Dewey's conception of "growth" is difficult to overstate. According to intellectual historian Richard Hofstadter, it has become a "source of endless difficulties" in education. Hofstadter adds that the Deweyan idea of "growth" has become "one of the most mischievous metaphors in the history of modern education."[8]

Dewey concedes the logical objections to his notion of growth by taking the part of his reader and asking, "Why, then, even supply [classroom] materials, since they are a source of some suggestion or another?" (EE, 71). He declines, however, to provide a serious response. Although Dewey may not take such objections seriously, they are reasonable, given the difficulty in which he leaves the teacher. To be sure, those who teach are charged with making sense out of the impulses and desires of the student by ensuring that these emotions are properly focused on useful objectives and are based upon productive strategies. But the teacher may not rely for guidance upon any settled educational principles, nor even foster recognized virtues as the disciplines by which students may pursue whatever it is that they should pursue. The teacher may do no more than casually suggest to students that they may have deviated from pursuing (undefined) goals, or that they might be employing inappropriate strategies to travel toward whatever horizons to which their impulses may aspire. According to Dewey, though, to exceed such minimalist guidance is "abuse" (EE, 71).

Consequently, Dewey's promotion of "intelligence" is reflected today in a misguided and sterile preoccupation with "critical thinking." Critical thinking has always been, and will continue to be, a by-product of a sound liberal arts education involving history, philosophy, logic, mathematics, and the like. There are no pedagogical shortcuts to sound thinking and those who reject a traditional canon deprive their students of the very tools they need to think well, notwithstanding their promise to teach pupils to "think for themselves." Critical thinking is the result of a sound education and nothing less.

Most curiously, programs of critical thinking skills frequently denigrate the accumulation of mere "information" on the assumption that "facts" have little to do with true intelligence. These programs unfortunately ignore the impossibility of acquiring sound judgment without historical and other relevant information. Alan Ryan notes that Dewey's contemporaries criticized him for the tendency to overemphasize "the problem of making children think, to the detriment of providing them with something to think about."[9] Ironically, the students educated in a Deweyan system will likely prove less "intelligent" and less capable of critical thinking than those students Dewey has not "emancipated" from the traditional classroom.

Indeed, the deprecation of knowledge in favor of "skills" constitutes one of the most illogical ideas animating contemporary educational theory. In taking such a position, educators try to separate what is inseparable, supposing that students can reason in a vacuum without having the basic information with which to reason. It is true, of course, that there are certain skills that should be taught if we want students to think critically. But the disciplines that teach these skills, such as rhetoric and informal logic, are nowhere to be found in Deweyan inspired curricula. A similar disdain attends to discussions of "rote-memorization" since such practices, as Dewey taught, only perpetuate "authoritarian" canons.

Dewey is enormously influential in educational thought, and such influence is no doubt due in part to the rich liberal arts education that he himself enjoyed, study that included Latin and Greek, philosophy, history, and an especially challenging literature curriculum. Deweyan scholar David Fott astutely asks whether such an education would have produced a John Dewey if Dewey had followed the kind of schooling that he later prescribed.[10]

Today's critical thinking programs all too often teach that "critical thinking" consists of adopting a particular ideologically charged "progressive" world view. This kind of mischievous socializing is today's incarnation of Dewey's so-called critical thinking. To be sure, just as Dewey was willing to let education serve his social ambitions, so also was he willing to redefine thinking itself as a kind of mental experimentation. He develops this proposal in *Logic: The Theory of Inquiry* (1903). This convenient depreciation of reasoning makes it difficult to call Dewey's ideas illogical. In his review of Dewey's work on logic, Charles Peirce, the father of American pragmatism, accused Dewey of "a debauch of loose reasoning" and "intellectual licentiousness."[11]

Goals, Objectives, and Hegemony

For Dewey, conventional "goals" are no more than adult prefer-ences. He believes, moreover, that goals and standards steal away a student's motivation because they are never perfectly attainable. It is in place of these allegedly abstract educational goals that Dewey offers his own (abstract) conception of growth. He insists, "Since in reality there is nothing to which growth is relative save more growth, there is nothing to which education is subordinate save more education" (DE, 50–51, 56–57). When Dewey cannot avoid speaking of measurements of schoolhouse progress, he prefers to speak of "aims" in education, rather than ideals or goals. But even so, if ideals are prohibited, at what does education "aim?" Dewey stipulates that whatever it might be, it can be decided only within the educational process; it cannot be imposed from without. There is no "end outside of the educative process to which education is subordinate" (DE, 100). Only educators can evaluate educators.

The teacher becomes a kind of pawn in Dewey's system, one who can impose no goals upon the pupil, for to do so would be "fatal" to real progress. The conventional system of "the assignment of lessons and the giving of directions by another," Dewey insists, is "nonsense." Dewey's "aims" may fluctuate: they must be tentative, "flexible," and subject to change just as a farmer alters his methods based upon changes in soil, climate, and weather conditions (DE, 104–5). Applied to education, this means that "it is as absurd for the [teacher] to set up his own aims as the proper objects of the growth of the children as it would be for the farmer to set up an ideal of farming irrespective of conditions." He further qualifies the subject by explaining that aims might be considered "suggestions" (DE, 107). Making the issue yet more obscure, he adds, "Educators have to be on their guard against ends that are alleged to be general and ulti-mate," because "'general'· also means 'abstract,'" and "such abstract-ness means remoteness, and throws us back, once more" (DE, 109).

Even "aims," then, make education irrelevant and autocratic, since they place the school's focus on "preparation for the future rather than living in the present" (DE, 110).[12]

American educational leaders today are deeply confused over standards and goals, even while these terms dominate their rhetoric. Such confusion seems a natural consequence of Dewey's insistence on such fluid educational standards. Educators seem to be locked in an interminable debate over the purpose of ordinary schooling and the proper means of measurement. Consequently, a steady progression of pedagogical standards or outcomes march across the educational landscape, some of which are quite imaginative, even if they are ultimately unhelpful and misleading.

Federal and state bureaucrats use those ideas to assert their hegemony over the business of teaching, exhausting the classroom professional who may actually be held accountable for the daily achievement of her students. This educational bureaucracy includes in its numbers a new mandarin class of "educational experts," without whose endorsement educational practice or reform cannot proceed. Surely we have entered into the theater of the absurd when educators cannot confidently teach a normal eight-year-old to read without reference to the latest "literature" on reading. The result of all this is children who do not read.

The absence of objective means of assessment—clear goals and standards—means that no one can assess education except the educators, who are the only legitimate interpreters of the new science of education. This in turn has fostered the cultivation of a self-contained "discipline" of education. As John Dykhuizen explains, it is Dewey who pioneered the separation of pedagogy into a discipline of its own, apart from subject matter.[13] When, inspired by Dewey's ideas, the progressive Teacher's College of Columbia University became autonomous from the university at large, it provided a telling symbol of the artificial separation of teaching *method* and teaching *substance*, with the consequential pursuit of the former and neglect of the latter. Educational historian Lawrence Cremin notes that this dichotomy led "to an inexorable divorce from the arts and sciences that tore asunder the teacher-preparing function of the university and increasingly insulated the work of the pedagogical faculty."[14]

Politics by Other Means

Earlier in this book, I noted that the integrity of Dewey's promise of better education is compromised in at least two ways. The first is Dewey's concern with progressive social reform, a preoccupation that justifies his desire to use the schools to transform society. In and of itself, this approach does not mean that students will be uneducated; it just means that the school is not designed, in the first instance, for academics. The academic priorities of pupils are subordinate to more important social goals. Second, Dewey's opposition to traditional and religious ideas colors his call for the teaching of "objective" critical thinking; yet, his own secularist prejudices make unlikely his capacity for dispassionate judgment. These two problems are especially evident in the last book he wrote, *Experience and Education* (1938). To be sure, the objective reader will find it difficult to look upon Dewey's *Experience and Education* kindly. Dewey is on the defensive by this time and it shows: he has generated considerable criticism against which he must defend himself. This book, he writes, was published "as a retort to all those who accused him of bringing American education to its knees (EE, 9)."[15]

In this work, Dewey finally confronts many of the philosophical and practical problems evident in his educational thought, but he is essentially unrepentant. Although some have interpreted this book as a repudiation of many of his earlier progressive ideas, educational historian Herbert Kliebard rightly describes *Experience and Education* as "simply a summing up of what he had been saying all along."[16] Dewey argues that either other reformers and practitioners have misunderstood his ideas or they have misapplied his theory; he further argues that more time is needed for the experimental method to achieve coherent classroom practice.[17]

Dewey does confess that it is "difficult to develop a philosophy of education"; yet, he warns against returning to the flawed if proven pedagogy of the past. He notes disapprovingly that "every movement in the direction of a new order of ideas and of activities . . . calls out, sooner or later, to a return to what appear to be simpler and more fundamental ideas and practices of the past" (EE, 5–6). Recourse to the past, however, is not a Deweyan option.

One must admire Dewey for his tenacity, especially in the face of the persistent complaint that after so much time, he has so little to offer to replace what progressivism has discarded. It is in responding to this complaint, however, that Dewey's self-described "experimentalism" is helpful. He can argue that incoherence is not a problem in itself, but rather justifies the need for more experimentation, observation, and data collection. The failures of Deweyan progressivism do not mean that progressive education should be abandoned; on the contrary, such failures signal the need for more progressive experimentation. This is precisely the vicious cycle in which American education is trapped. To understand this is to comprehend not only Dewey's strategy, but also a great deal of the activity of the educational community every since.

In facing his critics in *Experience and Education,* Dewey's strategy is a familiar one even to casual observers of contemporary politics. As early as his preface, he tries to adopt the posture of a peacemaker and elder statesman standing above the fray, denouncing "isms" and "labels" and "negativity." He urges his readers to think in terms of "Education" (as opposed to "education") as if "Education" were a Platonic ideal beyond philosophical disagreement (EE, 6). Although Dewey initially adopts a conciliatory tone and offers a kind of *via media* between extremes, within a few pages he abandons his apparent evenhandedness in order to provide yet another critique of all things traditional (EE, 17).[18]

One example of Dewey's disingenuous claim to impartiality in *Experience and Education* will suffice: in nonprogressive schools, Dewey complains, students are condemned to "essentially static" learning, burdened with "a finished product," and prohibited from "active participation." They are sentenced "to do and learn, as it was the part of the six hundred to do and die" (EE, 19). With this reference to Tennyson's "Charge of the Light Brigade," Dewey compares the situation of students in traditional classrooms to that of soldiers sent to die in what he no doubt believed to be a senseless slaughter. Given such a harsh attack on traditional education, how can we believe Dewey when he claims he is transcending partisanship?[19]

Thanks in no small part to Dewey, much of what characterizes contemporary education is a revolt against various expressions of authority: a revolt against a canon of learning, a revolt against tradition, a revolt against religious values, a revolt against moral standards, a revolt against logic—even a revolt against grammar and spelling. In many classrooms, the concern is whether sufficient authority exists simply to guarantee physical safety and survival. Dewey's revolt has carried American education to the place where he himself admitted he had arrived late in life: "I seem to be unstable, chameleon-like, yielding one after another to many diverse and even incompatible influences; struggling to assimilate something from each and yet striving to carry it forward."[20]

4

=

Democracy Betrayed

Educators, parents and students . . . must be induced to abandon the educational path that, rather blindly, they have been
following as a result of John Dewey's teachings.
                              — President Dwight D. Eisenhower

AMERICA IS REARING YOUNG PEOPLE WHO, to an alarming degree,
are historically illiterate. This according to the Department of Education's
2001 U.S. History National Assessment of Educational Progress (NAEP).[1]
In a press statement introducing the report, Secretary of Education Ron
Paige admitted that "too many of our public school children are still
struggling in this critical core subject area—history." "The higher the
grade in school," he added, "the lower their understanding in history."
He condemned the situation as "unacceptable" because it "is through
history that we understand our past and contemplate our future." "Our
shared history," he argued, "is what unites us as Americans." The
questions students can't answer, Paige reported, "involve the most
fundamental concepts of our democracy," a situation especially disconcerting "given the grave new world we've lived in since September 11th."
Finally, Paige anticipated those who would explain the problem solely
in terms of education financing: "Defenders of the status quo say it's not
enough money. Well, over the past fifty years, American taxpayers—at
the federal, state, and local levels—have spent trillions of dollars on our

schools and what have we got to show for it?" He then answered his own rhetorical question: "For starters—a third of our fourth graders who don't know that our fundamental right to 'life, liberty and the pursuit of happiness' comes from the Declaration of Independence."[2] The Center for Education Reform notes of this report, "American students are in a haze about their nation's history, and just as they are preparing to graduate high school and become contributing citizens, that haze becomes a thick, impenetrable fog."[3]

A similar study conducted by the American Council of Trustees and Alumni (ACTA) surveyed more than five hundred seniors at fifty-five top colleges and universities. The students were asked a series of multiple-choice questions on topics including the Magna Carta, the Monroe Doctrine, the Battle of Yorktown, and the Battle of the Bulge. Sixty-five percent of the students—from such prestigious schools as Yale, Northwestern, Smith, and Bowdoin—failed to pass the test and only one student answered all thirty-four questions correctly. Ninety-nine percent of the respondents, however, correctly identified the animated television characters Beavis and Butthead. Only 23 percent of the seniors identified James Madison as the "Father of the Constitution"; 98 percent, however, knew that Snoop Doggy Dog is a rapper.[4]

According to ACTA, "little more than half of college seniors know information about American democracy and the Constitution," and most "do not know specifics about major wars" in which the United States participated. Perhaps most startling is that no significant differences were found between the responses of history majors and those of students pursuing other disciplines.

Such historical ignorance, of which these reports are only a recent and partial indication, spurred House-Senate "Resolution on American History Education," which calls for the strengthening of American history requirements at all levels of the educational system. In proposing the resolution, Senator Joseph Lieberman warned,

"[O]ur next generation of leaders and citizens is leaving college with a stunning lack of knowledge of their heritage and the democratic values that have long sustained our country. . . . We cannot ignore the role of our public schools in contributing to this historical ignorance, so we must ask educators at all levels to redouble their efforts to bolster our children's knowledge of U.S. history and help us restore the vitality of our civic memory."[5] As syndicated columnist Mona Charen aptly asks, "If the words Yorktown, bleeding Kansas, reconstruction, Ellis Island, *Marbury vs. Madison,* 'Remember the Maine,' the Spirit of St. Louis, Midway, 'I shall return,' the Battle of the Bulge, the Hiss/Chambers case and 'Ich bin ein Berliner' mean no more to most Americans than to the average Malaysian, what is it that makes us Americans?"[6]

Dewey and Jefferson: Kindred Souls?

Should we be surprised at these survey results? After all, such historical illiteracy is indicative of Dewey's undisputed influence. Despite the fact that Dewey believed that he was the modern bearer of the educational torch once held by Thomas Jefferson, the foremost educational theorist of the founding generation, Dewey consciously revises the views of the founders while introducing radical innovations. This task is necessary, Dewey explains, in order to adapt the founders' democratic dream to the circumstances of the modern age. Their ideas, Dewey believes, though useful in the eighteenth century, were outworn and inadequate to sustain their hope of a successful republic. To the founders, a proper educational philosophy and practice is crucial to the success of the American nation—a principle with which Dewey agrees. But intentions aside, and contrary to the assertions of some scholars, Dewey's and Jefferson's educational approaches are radically different.[7]

Jefferson wrote far more on education than any other American leader of his generation. He argued that the proper education of the citizenry was vital to the health and longevity of the country that the founders had labored to establish. Other founders wrote and spoke extensively on education as well, most notably George Washington, Benjamin Rush, and Benjamin Franklin. Jefferson, however, is rightly regarded as the leading educational spokesman among the founders, because of the influence of both his educational theory and his practical recommendations. Since Dewey not only updates and departs from Jefferson's views, but also now supersedes Jefferson in influence, an understanding of the disagreement between Dewey and Jefferson is vital.

Of all the founders who wrote on education, Jefferson's thought occupies that shade of the spectrum closest to Dewey's progressive liberalism. For example, Jefferson anticipated in some measure, Dewey's optimism regarding progressive change and his belief that the superstitious and retrograde habits of the past could be overturned through rational enlightenment. Jefferson also was conspicuous among the founders in his belief in the advantages of, if not the occasional necessity for, political revolution. In such Jeffersonian ideas Dewey might find some support for his opposition to the American status quo. Finally, while he is not as militantly hostile to religious instruction as is Dewey, Jefferson did not, unlike some of his contemporaries, promote religion in the classroom, and he was clearly uncomfortable with the use of the Bible in the schools.

No surprise, then, that Dewey finds certain aspects of Jefferson's thought and character attractive. He wrote a small volume titled *The Living Thoughts of Thomas Jefferson* (1941), and he also discusses Jefferson's ideas in *Freedom and Culture* (1939). Although Dewey admits that Jefferson may have occasionally acted out of political expedience, he insists that Jefferson's actions were characterized, in the main, by unwavering principle. "[T]here are few men in public life whose course has been so straight," he writes. In Jefferson, claims

Dewey, "Natural sympathies, actual experiences, intellectual principles united to produce a character of a singular consistency and
charm." Indeed, Dewey holds the entire founding generation in a
certain kind of esteem: "There were giants in those days." He elaborates, "We may well be amazed, as well as grateful, at the spectacle of
the intellectual and moral caliber of the men who took a hand in
shaping the American political tradition" (TJ, 26, 4).

Dewey does not hesitate to identify those elements of Jefferson's
thought of which he approves. The first, of course, is Jefferson's
interest in education and his appreciation of the intimate tie between education and democracy. Second, Dewey appreciates
Jefferson's emphasis upon the popular sovereignty and natural equality of the people. It was "the 'people' in whom he trusted as the
foundation and ultimate security of self-governing institutions" (TJ,
11). Indeed, Dewey credits Jefferson with providing a necessary correction to the general course of American government by winning
the presidential election of 1800 and thus ending the Federalists'
hold on the executive office. He writes that "[Jefferson's] deep-
seated faith in the people and their responsiveness to enlightenment properly presented was a most important factor in enabling
him to effect, against great odds, 'the revolution of 1800.'" This
faith was the "cardinal element bequeathed by Jefferson to the
American tradition" (TJ, 18). Furthermore, Dewey also shares, to
some degree, Jefferson's concern that the growth of commercial
and industrial life undermined the nation's more wholesome and
vigorous agricultural virtues (QC, 282).

It appears, however, that what most strongly attracts Dewey
to Jefferson was the latter's inclination toward practical experimentation. One senses that, for Dewey, Jefferson's faith in experiment is
a precursor to Dewey's own wholly experimental philosophy. Dewey
speaks of Jefferson's "vital union of attitudes and convictions so spontaneous that they are of the kind called instinctive with fruits of a
rich and varied experience" (TJ, 3). He admires Jefferson's horti-
cultural, scientific, and architectural interests, probably because

Dewey thought they reflected his own sort of freewheeling intellectual style. He quotes approvingly Jefferson's observation that "the greatest service which can be rendered any country is to add a useful plant to its culture; especially, a bread grain; next in value to bread is oil" (TJ, 5).

Finally, Jefferson, like Dewey, was sensitive to and attracted by self-consciously progressive ideas. Jefferson had read the political writings of Rousseau (although whether he had read *Emile* is not known). He was aware of the educational theory of the eighteenth-century Swiss educational reformer Johann Heinrich Pestalozzi, whose mission was to implement Rousseau's theory as fully as possible. His observations on Pestalozzi indicate that Jefferson was open to different approaches to education, provided that they fulfilled his central objectives. Jefferson wrote to Joseph Carrington Cabell, a member of the Virginia senate and a political ally, "I have received information of Pestalozzi's mode of education from some European publications. . . . I sincerely wish it success, convinced that the information of the people at large can alone make them safe, as they are in the sole depository of our political and religious freedom."[8]

Educating Citizens and Leaders

For Jefferson, education should be directed toward two distinct groups: the average citizen and "those of superior ability for larger leadership and service."[9] He writes, "The greatest good [of the people] requires that while they are instructed in general, competently to the common business of life, others should employ their genius with necessary information to the useful arts, to invention for saving labor and increasing our comforts, to nourishing our health, to civil government, military science, etc." When Jefferson refers to this latter category of individuals, he is not referring to socioeconomic rank. He later speaks of a "natural aristocracy" but uses the word aristocracy in its original meaning—the "rule" (*kratos*) of the "excellent" or "virtuous" (*arete*). That this group is not defined socioeconomically is clear from his insistence that provision be made available to identify aristocratic talent among the poor. He sought the "talent which lies buried in poverty."[10]

In Jefferson's "Rockfish Gap Report" of 1818—the founding document of the University of Virginia—he elaborates on his belief that education must serve two distinct types: the citizen and the statesman. Primary education is to be aimed at the former and higher education at the latter: "The difference is clear: the citizen education is practical and turned toward private success, higher education is more philosophical and almost wholly directed to public service."[11] Although nature "has provided America with her share of genius, men of genius do not show themselves by nature at least in recognizable form, at least according to the ways by which prestige is usually awarded in society." Some persons, due to their circumstances, do not have the cultural advantages of higher society, nor do they have the financial means to pursue advanced education. Public education provides a mechanism by which disadvantaged yet virtuous individuals are located and enabled to pursue the vocation for which they are fitted. If the education of these individuals is subsidized, the country will give advanced education to all who are eligible, thus "mak[ing] the best use of its endowment" of genius for the public good. According to Jefferson's poignant if crude terminology, "the best geniuses will be raked from the rubbish annually."[12]

For Jefferson, a traditional liberal arts education plays an important role in building character. He contends that when a "moral sense" is underdeveloped in the student, "we endeavor to supply the defect by education." Specifically, he recommends the use of literature, telling his nephew, for example, to "read good books because they will encourage as well as direct your feelings."[13] As one Jefferson scholar explains, "Good books were to be read, not because of the doctrines they contained, but because of the encouragement and exercises which they gave the moral feelings."[14] The list of moral "habits" that good books encourage is long: they include gratitude, generosity, charity, kindness, truthfulness, a sense of justice, stability, organization, and courage.[15]

Jefferson also held the classical languages in high regard, both because of their intrinsic worth and because such study gave Jefferson himself the pleasure of enjoying classical literature throughout his life.[16] Generally, in all of Jefferson's curricular proposals, traditional liberal arts subjects like literature, music, philosophy, history, languages, and mathematics figure prominently at the elementary, secondary, or college level.[17]

The Paradox of Democratic Education

The challenge of civic education persistently demanded the attention of the founding generation. In the late eighteenth century, the American Philosophical Society even sponsored a contest offering a one-hundred-dollar prize for the essay that best described a system of education most suitable for the promotion and preservation of the new American republic.[18]

For Thomas Jefferson, the civic purpose of education presented a paradox: On the one hand, education must foster the capacity for critical judgment through a program of general study, with special emphasis upon the acquisition of knowledge, especially historical knowledge. On the other hand, students should acquire some measure of veneration for their own country. Thus, civic education involves a tension between the competing concepts of revolution and tradition. Fresh from an engagement with tyranny, the founders believed a republican education must sensitize the citizen to maintain a revolutionary's watchfulness, to guard his rights, and to recognize any attempts to undermine republican government. Yet for the sake of the stability of the regime, the citizen must also have a patriotic attachment to his country. Jefferson called this attachment to one's country "prejudice," and he even went so far as to discourage education abroad, where the student was likely to acquire "anti-republican" sentiments.[19] To be sure, although Noah Webster deprecated personal "pride," he recommended that students acquire a certain "national pride" in their country.[20]

This belief that education must instill patriotism was reiterated a generation later by Abraham Lincoln in one of his early public speeches, the "Address before the Young Men's Lyceum of Springfield, Illinois" delivered on January 27, 1838. Lincoln asked his audience, now two generations removed from the founding era, how the country might "fortify" itself against losing its precious political inheritance. His solution was to foster in children a patriotic "state of feeling" and to transmit an unapologetic inculcation in the laws and government of the nation. Lincoln proposes, "Let reverence for laws, be breathed by every American mother, to the lisping babe, that prattles on her lap—let it be taught in schools, in seminaries, and in colleges; let it be written in Primers, spelling books, and in Almanacs."[21]

In short, the task facing the educational theorists of the early American republic was to reconcile the enjoyment of liberty with the demands of order. The founders understood that the marriage of liberty and order was essential if the historically evanescent character of republics was to be overcome. An especially important component of republican education was the study of history. The preamble to Jefferson's "Bill for the More General Diffusion of Knowledge" asserts that education is the best means to maintain a government that protects the rights of its citizens. Jefferson believed, moreover, that history teaches that even the best governments are prone to degenerate, even if by slow steps, into autocratic regimes. The safeguard is to raise the consciousness and quality of judgment of the citizens through the study of history.[22] History is "indispensable" for a proper American education because otherwise students will not properly understand the danger posed by tyranny, whether that tyranny be autocratic or democratic.

Jefferson thought that human nature was, generally speaking, unchanging. For that reason, ancient history was as relevant as modern history.[23] Jefferson was convinced that a core curriculum involving meaningful historical studies was an integral foundation for the survival of republicanism itself. History had the potential to teach moral and civic lessons that would fortify the moral character of students as well as their civic character. In one instance, Jefferson recommended in particular "Graecian, Roman, English, and American history," subjects that characterized secondary education until they were supplanted by "social studies."[24]

Dewey's Departure from Jefferson

The closer the comparison between Dewey's and Jefferson's thought, the more evident are the ways in which Dewey departs from Jefferson and the rest of the founders on education. First, Jefferson is far more suspicious of human nature than is Dewey. Neither Jefferson in particular nor the founders in general shared Dewey's belief in the suppleness of human nature. They refused to rely on the present goodness or future perfectibility of man to secure their government or to base public education on such a premise. Dewey, by contrast, rejects the idea that human nature is fixed, believing instead that human action and qualities are largely determined by surrounding social forces. He cannot, therefore, put much stock in such ideas as character and personal virtue. Traditional character formation is far too individualistic for Dewey and is likely, he argues, to promote egoists not committed to social change. Character formation is also "undemocratic" because to promote character requires that the authority of the "parent, teacher, or textbook" be imposed upon the helpless student, who has little to say in the matter. Such a student is a victim, not a pupil.

Nor does Dewey subscribe to the notion that different sorts of education ought to be provided for citizens and for political leaders. In all of his educational writing, training for the leader and the citizen is one and the same enterprise, directed at all individuals without discrimination. Any other educational model is inappropriate for a democratic way of life. This is one of the reasons for his opposition to any kind of meaningful vocational education: he is afraid its very availability might subordinate its students to those who receive a more academic education.[25] Accordingly, Dewey believes that in a true democracy every student "must be educated for leadership as well as for obedience" (MPE, 10). Given that Dewey was more aware than are many today of the aristocratic dimensions of Jefferson's educational ideas, we must regard his egalitarianism as a self-conscious rejection of the attention Jefferson gives to a select group of potential leaders. At best, Dewey is indifferent to this important Jeffersonian distinction. In Dewey's school the student with superior potential may not advance without the less capable student as this would produce "inequality." The superior student then will inevitably be confined to a lower level of accomplishment. Consequently, the aristocratic talent Jefferson considered critical to good government will be drowned in a sea of mediocrity.

Furthermore, whereas Jefferson counts on the study of literature, history, language, and philosophy as a means of promoting moral, intellectual, and civic virtue, Dewey has little interest in such an education because he thinks it has no practical value. Perhaps more to the point, Dewey understands that liberal learning is, in an important sense, *traditional* and that it relies upon an authoritative canon. For Dewey, this is reason enough to exclude the liberal arts from the classroom. Though for the founders a liberal education is an important means of promoting moral character, Dewey has no use for such a curriculum. He sees it, at best, as obsolete and irrelevant; at worst, as an insidious hindrance to the realization of social change.

Finally, in contrast to Jefferson, Dewey discounts the educational value of "knowledge," especially historical knowledge. He is unwilling to trust the average citizen to understand or intelligently respond to historical and contemporary events. Dewey wrote that an "outstanding" example of the inability of the founders to grasp the wider context of democracy was "their faith in the public press and in schooling" (FC, 41). The founders, he argues, underestimated the power of propaganda and the inability of the average citizen to resist it. They "failed to see how," as in Germany in the twentieth century, mere "education in literacy could become a weapon in the hands of an oppressive government," or how "the chief cause for promotion of elementary education in Europe would be an increase in military power" (FC, 41). Dewey argues that despite the efficiency of the schools in Germany, they nonetheless "furnished the intellectual fodder for totalitarian propaganda" (FC, 41). He goes on to argue that the failure of the American school has been severe, even after Jefferson's dream of universal education was realized by the Common School movement in the middle of the nineteenth century. In other words, the founders' faith in the intelligence and judgment of the average citizen is not only misplaced; it leaves the country vulnerable to tyranny because the basic education promoted by the founders does not equip citizens to distinguish between facts and lies (FC, 42).

According to Dewey, literacy puts at the citizen's disposal little more than fragmented, sensational news stories and meaningless, abstract generalizations. The citizen cannot be expected to acquire meaningful knowledge or adequate judgment through his schooling. Dewey has little faith, then, in the important Jeffersonian belief in the ability of the properly educated citizen to judge public affairs competently. Dewey has no confidence that students can develop the facility to assimilate, analyze, and evaluate unedited political and social information. He argues that conventional educational practices leave the student ill equipped to resist "propaganda"; at best he is no more than a passive recipient of superficial and unorganized information.

Jefferson, by contrast, has far more confidence in an adequately educated citizenry. He explains the importance of giving such citizens "full information of their affairs through the channel of the public papers" as a means of checking the abuse of government. He continues, "The basis of our government being the opinion of the people . . . , were it left to me to decide whether we should have a government without newspapers, or newspapers without a government, I should not hesitate a moment to prefer the latter."[26]

Whereas Jefferson thought history a rich store of lessons and instruction, Dewey saw value in historical studies only if they could be made immediately relevant to the present—a difficult demand to satisfy. The only "moral significance" of history is its narrow use to cultivate "socialized intelligence." Precisely what Dewey intended historical studies to contain is not clear, but he does implicitly criticize Jefferson's belief that historical examples are vital for moral instruction:

> It is possible to employ [history] as a kind of reservoir of anecdotes to be drawn on to inculcate special moral lessons on this virtue or that vice. But such teaching is not so much an ethical use of history as it is an effort to create moral impressions by means of more or less authentic material. At best, it produces a temporary emotional glow; at worst, callous indifference to moralizing. (DE, 217)

By contrast, Jefferson intended just such a use of history, because it teaches valuable moral object lessons. He found traditional history classes exceptionally "relevant." In his words, "History by apprising [students] of the past will enable them to judge of the Future."[27] Jefferson no doubt would have seen Dewey's depreciation of history as antithetical to democratic education.

Jefferson might argue that to achieve a proper civic education is the most challenging educational problem of all, for the
citizen must be taught simultaneously to revere and to criticize
his government, neither allowing his patriotism to soften his judgment nor permitting his criticism to weaken his civic pride. For
Dewey, however, there is no tension in civic education. Any notion of attachment to one's country is forgotten in his zeal for
social, if not political, change. The founders labored to lay a foundation for civic education that had as its goal the permanence of
American structures and processes. Dewey, by contrast, wants
schools to lead a revolt—not one aimed at realigning the citizen's
heart and mind with the accomplishments of 1776, but one aimed
at a social and economic revolution that would undermine them.
Dewey displays a careless disregard for the tough task of maintaining structural and procedural stability. He questions the
importance of the American system of voting rights and wonders
whether "some functional organization would not serve to for-
mulate and manifest public opinion better than the existing
methods."[28] In the same context he can question the need for the
nation-state while simultaneously suggesting that it assume the
role of orchestrating both public and private affairs (RP, 202–3).
Indeed, Dewey curiously dismisses a preoccupation with the "established mechanisms" of American government as a kind of
"idolatry of the Constitution" (FC, 158).

The Utility of Ideals

Dewey argues that since ideals are not perfectly attainable, they
may demoralize students who try to measure up to them. But
Jefferson would argue that Dewey's unwillingness to accept any
transcendent principles jeopardizes the very process of social
reform that he so highly prizes. In contrast with Dewey, Jefferson
does not dismiss abstract moral principles as hindrances to
pragmatic social change. They are, to the contrary, prerequisites

to improvement, for they serve as the ideals that inspire individuals to push beyond the boundaries of the contemporary status quo. They are goals at which to aim, indispensable supports for resolve against moral vacillation. Belief, for example, in a transcendent and unalterable concept of "justice" inspires and motivates the social reformer to seek a more "just" society. Ideals also provide a critical lens through which to judge contemporary values and norms and thus serve as a measure of social progress.

For that reason, Jefferson includes in his most important document, the Declaration of Independence, an early statement of ideals: "We hold these *truths* to be self-evident. . . ." Not only did Jefferson's appeal to principle inspire and legitimize the American Revolution, these principles have provided the tools of an ongoing assessment of the country's progress toward its citizens' enjoyment of equality and liberty. Lincoln noted Jefferson's claim that all are "created equal" when he praised the Declaration: "All honor to Jefferson—to the man who, in the concrete pressure of a struggle for national independence by a single people, had the coolness, forecast and capacity to introduce into a merely revolutionary document, an abstract truth, applicable to all men and all times."[29]

Despite Jefferson's well-known anticlericalism and heterodoxy, he nonetheless recognizes that not only were ideals essential, but he also concedes that they may be rooted in some conception of divine justice. Referring to the institution of slavery in the early nineteenth century, Jefferson suggests that such inhumane abuse may somehow and at some time result in calamity. He asserts, "The seeds of hatred and revenge which present oppressors are now sowing with a large hand, will not fail to produce their fruits in time. Like their brother robbers on the highway, they suppose the escape of the moment a final escape, and deem infamy and future risk countervailed by present gain."[30] Elsewhere, in a famous passage later cited by Abraham Lincoln in reference to the American Civil War, Jefferson ruefully asks, "And can the liberties of a nation be thought secure when we have removed their only firm basis, a conviction in the minds of the people that these liberties are of the gift of God? That they are not to be violated but with his wrath? Indeed I tremble for my country when I reflect that God is just."[31]

Dewey, by contrast, explicitly rejects the foundation of the Declaration of Independence. He suggests that the philosophical principles that underlie that document "have gone out of vogue." "Self-evident truths," moreover, "have been weakened by historic and by philosophic criticism" (FC, 156). Modern conditions mean that the general principles upon which the country was founded no longer have "practical meaning." They are now no more than "emotional cries" (PP, 133).

Dewey and the "Real World"

In his many writings and political activities, Dewey was fiercely opposed to capitalism and hostile—at least in theory—to the unregulated possession of private property. Dewey condemns a government that maintains and fosters "the private property of predatory and stupidly selfish interests."[32] He was, moreover, not simply a modern liberal but a thoroughgoing socialist who favored government ownership of industry wherever it was feasible and extensive regulation where it was not, although, for practical reasons, he never supported the American Socialist Party. Dewey's greatest apologist, Sidney Hook, explains that Dewey's so-called Depression book, *Individualism—Old and New* (1930), marks the author's break with capitalism and acceptance of socialism.[33] Dewey's political-economic preference is a point on which we might find reasonable disagreement. His attempt to use the school to propagate the same, however, is a more serious matter. Equally troubling, at least from a philosophical point of view, is that Dewey's experimentalism does not offer any clear principles on which a government might be based, and by which the dignity of the individual, his family, and his private associations might be secured.

Drawing an analogy by which he would later be embarrassed, Dewey wrote in 1939 that the United States should take a lesson from "the state of things in totalitarian countries" (FC, 9). These countries realized that to effect revolutionary change one must consider, and seek to influence, all facets of the country's culture through education. In this respect, Dewey readily admits his departure from the founders' thought: "The import of this conclusion extends far beyond its contrast with the simpler faith of those who formulated the democratic traditions" (FC, 13).

In the summer of 1928, Dewey received an invitation from the Soviet Union's education minister to lead a group of educators on a visit to the U.S.S.R. Jay Martin reports the enthusiasm with which the Soviets received Dewey's educational ideas.

> In Moscow Dewey attended a conference organized by Professor A. G. Kalashnikov of the pedagogical department Moscow Technical University. Ten days later Kalashnikov sent Dewey a two-volume set of the *Soviet Pedagogical Encyclopedia* for 1927, with a note: "Your works, especially 'School and Society' and 'The School and the Child,' have very much influenced the development of the Russian pedagogy and in the first years of [the] revolution you were one of the most renowned writers." "At present," he continued, "Soviet "philosophico-socialist [sic]" theory differed a bit from Dewey's recommendations, but still, those "concrete shapes of pedagogical practice, which you have developed in your works, will be for a long time the aim of our tendencies."[34]

Such an unwelcome endorsement does not seem to worry Martin, who defends Dewey from the implications of this communication by insisting that Dewey always made a distinction between the Russian people, whom he admired, and "Marxist theory and Soviet politics," of which he always disapproved.[35] But this distinction was lost on most of Dewey's critics at the time. Even

Dewey himself later admitted that his misunderstanding of Soviet political dynamics was "shameful."[36]

Nevertheless, Dewey consistently displays a lack of appreciation for the institutional and procedural features of authentically democratic life. His thought and politics, moreover, are often influenced by his dissatisfaction with American political and economic culture. Except perhaps in its ideals, Dewey thought America a poor example for the other countries in which he showed political interest—for example, China, Turkey, Mexico, and the Soviet Union. He believed that American society had become outdated, since it was now driven not merely by "rugged individualism," which for Dewey was at best obsolete, but by a degenerative form of the same, which he called "ragged individualism," or aggressive greed incited by opportunistic big business.[37] In place of this system Dewey issues vague but insistent calls for better "communication" and "community." In practice, these terms are code words for a pollyannish view of human nature and for a belief in the social superiority of the properly managed school to the family.[38]

Dewey yearns for the emergence and development of something he calls "the public," which will make life more humane. He is unable, however, to explain just what the public is, or what it should look like should it emerge from its present "inchoate" condition (PP, 109). At present, the public is "lost" and "bewildered," but if it can be nurtured, it will become the new center of gravity for democracy, displacing the individual (PP, 116). The key to saving the "public" is "better debate, discussion and persuasion" (PP, 208).[39] However superficially appealing this rhetoric may be, it begs the question of what structures and processes support civic dialogue, and what principles might better foster communication. Dewey's call for communication also ignores the investigation of those intrinsic qualities of human nature which frustrate or facilitate better communication. Nor is he clear about what, precisely, citizens must communicate better.

Although we may sympathize with Dewey's longings for a more humane society, it is difficult to take his discussions of politics seriously. Sometimes those discussions are, in a word, absurd: "And when the emotional force, the mystic force one might say, of communication, of the miracle of shared life and shared experience is spontaneously felt, the hardness and crudeness of contemporary life will be bathed in the light that never was on land or sea" (RP, 211). To be sure, Dewey has no real political philosophy at all and may not have appreciated the need for one. He almost always speaks in terms of "social policy" rather than political philosophy, even though the establishment of the latter must precede the development of the former (see, e.g., RP, 187ff).

Political philosophy or no political philosophy, Dewey is committed to using education to revolutionize American society, if not the American system of government. In *Schools of Tomorrow*, employing language now familiar, Dewey complains that heretofore schools have been based upon unjust social arrangements created for the advantage of a few and the disadvantage of the many. The schools, he writes, were designed and developed in a pre-revolutionary era. Strangely, though, when he speaks of "revolution" he has in mind the French Revolution. He curiously identifies American education with the social class abuses and deprivation characteristic of pre-revolutionary France, ignoring its differences with pre-revolutionary America. Indeed, Dewey seems to believe that the United States still languishes in a kind of pre-revolutionary period, the events of 1776 notwithstanding.

Many of today's progressive educators are likely to resist the ideas of the founders because such traditional educational philosophy is "reactionary." Progressive education, however, both in its historical and contemporary guises, is far more reactionary than the traditions it attacks. Political scientist J. Martin Rochester rightly notes, "Many of today's progressives who criticize traditionalists as 'back to basics' dinosaurs are themselves merely going back in time and recycling earlier theories advanced by John Dewey and others."⁴⁰ Those involved in education reform know this all too well: entrenched educational bureaucrats and activists may be so oppositional that they adamantly resist even reasonable discussion of ideas contrary to their own.

In his incisive indictment of American education, *The Closing of the American Mind*, Allan Bloom notes that Dewey "regarded our history as irrelevant or as a hindrance to rational analysis of our present."⁴¹ Bloom rues the damage Dewey's thought has done to the all-important activity of civic education: "John Dewey taught us that the only danger confronting us is being closed to the emergent, the new, the manifestations of progress. No attention had to be paid to . . . fundamental principles or . . . virtues." "Civic culture," Bloom concludes, "was neglected."⁴²

Dewey was more aware than most of his contemporary defenders of just how sharply he deviated from Jefferson's ideas while still finding it useful to invoke Jefferson's memory. In *Freedom and Culture,* he anticipates the complaints that he had misappropriated Jefferson's authority, writing, "I make no apology for linking what is said . . . with the name of Thomas Jefferson" (FC, 155). Perhaps he should have apologized, though, because it is difficult to find any way in which Dewey's radical changes improved upon the sound ideas and practices of the "giants" of the eighteenth century, as Dewey himself regarded them. In the end, although Dewey found Jefferson a convenient authority to whom to appeal in support of his progressive ideas, any similarities between the educational thought of the two men are superficial, while the differences are crucial. Dewey subverts the educational intentions of Jefferson and of the entire founding generation. In light of the founders' aspirations, Dewey's schoolhouse revolution compromises the integrity of American leadership, deprecates moral and civic virtue, depreciates the importance of constitutional structures and processes, and thus undermines the well-being of the American republic.

5
=

A Useful Education

An excellent man would deal in noble fashion with poverty,
disease, and other sorts of bad fortune.   —Aristotle

IN "LEAF BY NIGGLE," J. R. R. TOLKIEN TELLS the beautiful
story of an amateur artist of mediocre talent who ultimately learns that
his artistic efforts find their fullest expression only after he has learned
the priority of neighborly charity. Niggle, the artist, further discovers
that all of his seemingly pointless creative ambitions find profound
completion in an afterlife. After his death, two town officials debate the
merit of Niggle's activity. Their discussion centers on the "usefulness"
of Niggle's life. Councillor Tompkins complains to Atkins the school-
teacher that Niggle's life was in the end not useful at all. "'I think he was
a silly little man,' said Councillor Tompkins. 'Worthless, in fact; no use
to society at all.'" The school teacher, on the other hand, suggests that
Tompkins's definition of "usefulness" is too cramped. "'Oh, I don't
know,' said Atkins. . . . 'I am not sure. It depends on what you mean by
use.'"

Tompkins further complains that Niggle had no "practical or
economic use." He could have been a "serviceable cog of some sort,"
Tompkins continues, "if you schoolmasters knew your business." If
Tompkins had had has his way, he explains, he would have put him to

work "in a communal kitchen or something." Otherwise, he would have been "put away."

"Then you don't think painting is worth anything, not worth preserving, or improving, or even making use of?" asks Atkins. At this point, the crass nature of Tompkins's concept of "utility" is revealed:

> "Of course painting has uses," said Tompkins. "But you couldn't make use of his painting. There is plenty of scope for bold young men not afraid of new ideas and new methods. None of this old-fashioned stuff. Private day-dreaming. He could not have designed a telling poster to save his life. Always fiddling with leaves and flowers. I asked him why, once. He said he thought they were pretty! Can you believe it? He said *pretty*! 'What, digestive and genital organs of plants?' I said to him; and he had nothing to answer."[1]

This story recalls another Tolkien passage, this time from *The Hobbit*, in which the narrator takes a dim view of goblins precisely because their life is driven by an exaggerated and thus deformed kind of utility. He explains, "Now goblins are cruel, wicked, and bad-hearted. They make no beautiful things, but they make many clever ones."[2]

The question of how "useful" an education should be is an old debate. Over two millennia ago, Aristotle lamented that "[i]nvestigation on . . . education yields confusion, and it is not at all clear whether one should have training in things useful for life, or things contributing to virtue."[3] In the nineteenth century, some years before the heyday of progressive education, John Henry Newman addressed the false dichotomy often posed between a useful and a liberal education. The chief goal of education, Newman argued, should be to produce a healthy intellect. A healthy intellect, moreover, is analogous to a healthy body. Without it, there is little one can do that is lasting and useful; with it, an individual is capable of great things.

A healthy mind is an indispensable prerequisite to any kind of professional success or social effectiveness. Newman notes that "educated men" are those who have "learned to think and to reason and to compare and to discriminate and to analyze." The educated man has "formed his judgment, and sharpened his mental vision." Such an individual has developed "that state of intellect" necessary for the entering of a profession. He will be a better businessman, soldier, or engineer than his comparatively uneducated counterpart because— by virtue of his education—he is a better human being.[4] A sound general education gives the student "an ease, a grace, a versatility"— qualities essential to success in his or her undertakings. Such an education, Newman maintains, "is emphatically *useful*."[5]

In Newman's eloquent phrase, a humane education "is the great ordinary means to a great but ordinary end." The objectives of such an education are ambitious: they include "raising the intellectual tone of society," "cultivating the public mind," "facilitating the exercise of political power," and "refining the intercourse of private life." Armed with an authentic general education, a student can "fill any post with credit" and "master any subject with facility."[6]

But these advantages do not accrue because an education is designed, in the first place, to be *useful*, but rather only if it is designed to be *good*, that is, only if it builds on the great tradition of liberal learning consisting of the canons of art, history, literature, philosophy, science, and mathematics—all of which contribute to the intellectual, moral, and spiritual formation of the student. Newman explains that a "good" education is always useful, because what is good will inevitably lead to further good: "I say, let us take 'useful' to mean, not what is simply good, but what *tends* to good, or is the *instrument* of good; and in this sense also . . . I will show you how a liberal education is truly and fully a useful, though it be not a professional, education."[7] The "good," Newman continues, "is not only good, but reproductive of good" because it spreads its likeness "all around." He concludes, "A great good will impart great good" to the world. A good education "must necessarily be useful too."[8]

Similarly, Aristotle criticizes the education of the Spartans precisely because their education was directed only toward "necessary and useful things," with little regard for what is "noble."[9] In this light, it is notable that although historians grant the Spartans the respect they are due for their martial discipline, the same historians also note that the Spartans left no philosophical, literary, or political legacy, unlike their Athenian rivals.

Here we have a paradox: In making utility the chief goal of education, we sacrifice much of its usefulness. A merely utilitarian education is largely ineffectual precisely because it does not seek to make a student good, or at least to teach him what is good, or even to provide him with those principles that guide good behavior—all of which qualities are essential aspects of true utility. Jaime Castiello notes that if a man were to raise cattle over a gold mine, his farm would be "serving a useful purpose" but would yield "greater profits if used in other ways." Applying the analogy to education, he explains, "The weakness of the so-called utilitarian attitude is that it is not sufficiently utilitarian: it disregards, and therefore wastes, the most precious educational values and consequently it resembles the conduct of the man who would use mining land for pasture."[10] By contrast, he asserts, a humane or liberal education "includes everything which is desired by the utilitarian and much more."[11]

A Love of Truth and Learning

Aristotle explains that truly great men and women are inspired by principles more expansive than those guiding a particular professional pursuit or closely defined social objective. He teaches in the *Politics* that a good citizen, one who is loyal to the constitution and government, is not automatically a good man, for a good man inevitably would oppose his regime and its political practices if these were unjust. It is only in the very best regime—perhaps only in an ideal regime—that the virtue of a good man and a good citizen intersect, since a perfect social order would need no loyal opposition from its citizens.[12]

Aristotle further argues that if one is truly interested in social reform, one must strive for general excellence in education. This is because, just as Newman argued, individuals of excellence will spread their excellence around. Aristotle writes, "An excellent man would deal in noble fashion with poverty, disease, and other sorts of bad fortune."[13] On the other hand, without noble people it is unclear who will be equipped with the very virtues needed in the fight for social change. The civil rights movement in this country illustrates well why ideals that transcend the moral status quo are essential for improvement. Martin Luther King Jr. drew upon, for example, the prophet Isaiah's beautiful image of "justice flowing" like water to stir opposition to racial discrimination in his "I Have a Dream" speech. Ironically, then, prospects for real social improvement are constricted if students are not taught that there are principles above and beyond "utility." The justice of a society is directly proportional to the inspirational ideals with which students are equipped, and that philosophical equipping must necessarily occur in schools, as well as in churches and homes.

Accordingly, the nineteenth-century educational reformer Horace Mann argued that education must elevate students to appreciate those high principles that should guide personal life and inspire social improvement. "Education is to inspire the love of truth," he wrote, "as the supremest good, and to clarify the vision of the intellect to discern it. We want a generation of men above deciding great and eternal principles upon narrow and selfish grounds." Education, Mann insisted, should promote a "love of truth."[14]

Aristotle and Plato drew their conclusions about the education of youth from the major premise that a student has a soul. Indeed, Aristotle suggests that anyone involved in designing and guiding educational institutions "must study the soul."[15] Though the soul cannot be measured or analyzed by conventional means, Aristotle admonishes us not to demand more precision in what we study than the subject matter will yield.[16] Educators today tend to be preoccupied with "assessments" and the measurement of "outcomes"; they would do well to moderate such pursuits with a renewed appreciation for the student's inner life.[17] Otherwise, they may ignore what Aristotle calls "the first principle of living things."[18]

Even though the human soul does not yield to prevailing means of investigation, the intelligent educator will recognize that those things that cannot be measured may be, ironically, the core of a meaningful and truly good education. A basic understanding of the soul, for example, guided the Greek philosophers in determining when education should attempt to form the ethics of students through moral training, and when the appeal should be made to reason. Aristotle's philosophy would suggest that such judgments—critical for the pursuit of a sound civic and moral education—cannot be made reliably if the student is regarded as little more than flesh, blood, and designer jeans. Plato explains that the central thrust of education must be to cultivate intellectual and moral virtue because "virtue . . . would be a certain health, beauty, and good condition of a soul"; without an education directed to the soul, the student will be left with "vice" which is "a sickness, ugliness and weakness" of the soul.[19]

No doubt much of this sounds quaint to modern ears, for the materialistic assumption of progressive education rules out the possibility that a meaningful education must draw a student's attention away from the immediate to the transcendent. Such an appeal must concern itself with questions of beauty, nobility, and goodness, whether the appeal is made through religion, philosophy, art, music, or literature. A soulful education, moreover, cannot be structured around ever-changing questions of social relevance or transitory political fads. Rather, it must heed Plutarch's warning that the education of youth must not be misdirected into "vulgar twaddle."[20] A materialistic education produces materialists, so many J. Alfred Prufrocks, whose biggest daily decision, T. S. Eliot explains, is where to part their hair.

Thus, education must do more than teach rudimentary skills— even though many today would be satisfied with mere verbal and numerical literacy. It must also inspire students and enable them to discriminate between what is meaningful and what is superficial, between what is noble and what is crude. It must provide them with nutrition for the soul, a repository from which to draw for strength upon graduation, as well as the power to discriminate between what is decent and what is degrading. In this respect, J. R. R. Tolkien's idea of "waybread" is helpful. In *The Return of the King*, Tolkien explains the importance of the elves' bread, with its power to sustain Sam and Frodo as they come ever closer to Mount Doom on their increasingly arduous quest to destroy the Ring:

> The *lembas* had a virtue without which they would long ago have lain down to die. It did not satisfy desire, and at times Sam's mind was filled with the memories of food, and the longing for simple bread and meats. And yet this waybread of the Elves had a potency that increased as travelers relied on it alone and did not mingle it with other foods. It fed the will, and it gave strength to endure, and to master sinew and limb beyond the measure of mortal kind.[21]

Education should provide a kind of "waybread" to students for their journey through life, a storehouse of knowledge, ideals, principles, and stories upon which they can draw. Tolkien's waybread is not designed simply to "satisfy desire," nor should the waybread of the curriculum gratify the transitory whims of students; rather, it should aim to provide the life-giving sustenance necessary to choose goals wisely, to endure hardship tenaciously, and to direct the passions appropriately.

It has been argued that a good education is what a student has left when he has forgotten everything he has learned. This occurs when the student learns for the sake of learning, not just to achieve a useful goal. "All men by nature desire understanding," wrote Aristotle, but at perhaps no time in history has there existed such apathy in the schools.[22] Drawing much from Dewey, modern attempts to cater to students' interests and make education "relevant" seem to have backfired. It seems time to attend again to the likes of Michel de Montaigne, who explains that "there is nothing like tempting the boy to want to study and to love it. . . . Learning must not only lodge with us: we must marry her."[23]

Benjamin Franklin on a Pragmatic Education

Benjamin Franklin's educational ideas pushed the limits of what a pragmatic education might be, yet he did not eschew the educational inheritance of which he was the beneficiary. Franklin's "realist"—if not iconoclastic—approach to education sought to provide a new educational model for the youth of Pennsylvania, one that would be geared to their practical success. He suggested, for example, as did Dewey more than a century later, that a student's interest might, at times, serve as the cue for introducing him to a particular discipline. Franklin, moreover, was not only critical of the predominant secondary and university education of his day, but on one occasion attacked it with biting satire through his literary persona Silence Dogwood.[24] To a correspondent he stated flatly that schools "proceed upon false principles" and aim "at a false mark."[25]

Franklin disdained the abstract in favor of the concrete. Thomas Woody explains that Franklin's mind was regularly "drawn, as if by a powerful magnet, to some earthy, practical, perplexing problem."

Whirlwinds, waterspouts, balloons, stoves, the Gulf Stream, electrical fire, smoking chimneys, optics, medicine, finance,

sundials, tides, absorption and reflection of heat, military
science, silk culture, gardening, scientific agriculture, meteo-
rology, and hydrostatics were among the things that interested him and to many of which he gave studious hours when
not printing books, selling them, or serving in public offices.

But, writes Woody, although "[u]tility was his first criterion; to do
good [was] his purpose."[26] Accordingly, Franklin encouraged innovation, recommending at times unconventional methods of pedagogy. This attitude derived no doubt from the unique ways in which
he himself was educated, an education that was largely autodidactic.
For example, he failed to learn mathematics in school and so later
taught himself using a primer of the day, Cocker's *Arithmetic*.[27]

Franklin proposed an "English academy" in which ancient
languages, and at times even modern foreign languages, would be
eliminated or at least postponed in favor of making students mas-
ters of the vernacular. He suggested that students, if they studied
Latin at all, might find it most useful to do so *after* modern foreign
languages, rather than before. In this way, students might then appreciate the degree to which Latin is the foundation of the Romance
languages and why it merits their attention. Even at that, however,
he thought that a study of ancient languages might not be useful for
many students if it were not relevant to their prospective professions. Indeed, he once argued that many educational practices were
like clothing styles—though they once might have served a purpose, they were often thoughtlessly retained when no longer needed.

In spite of Franklin's attraction to the useful and the innovative, however, he, like Jefferson, believed the moral goal of education to be the promotion of personal virtue. He once advised a friend
in regard to character development: "Be studious in your profession, and you will be learned. Be industrious and frugal, and you
will be rich. Be sober and temperate, and you will be healthy. Be in
general virtuous, and you will be happy." Franklin's own list of virtues to which he aspired included "Temperance, Silence, Order,

Resolution, Frugality, Industry, Sincerity, Justice, Moderation, Cleanliness, Tranquility, and Chastity." He later added "Humility" when a Quaker friend told him he was generally regarded to be proud, though he admitted that he found its cultivation elusive.[28]

Though Franklin was not conventionally pious, he was by no means an enemy of traditional belief or institutionalized religious observance. Included in his diary, kept for reasons of personal inspiration, was a line from Addison's popular play *Cato*:

> Here will I hold. If there's a power above us
> (And that there is, all nature cries aloud
> Through all her works), He must delight in virtue;
> And that which He delights in must be happy.[29]

Though Franklin found it hard to attend the church services of his day, he nonetheless and with apparent sincerity advocated it for the young. He wrote his daughter Sally, admonishing her to "constantly" attend church, whether she liked the preacher or not. He admired the Common Prayer Book and recommended it as an "act of devotion." Such devotion, he wrote, should constitute Sally's "principal business" in attending church. The prayer book, moreover, would be useful in "amending the heart," since the prayers therein "were composed by men of much greater piety and wisdom than our common composers of sermons can pretend to be, and therefore I wish you would never miss the prayer days."[30]

Franklin followed a practice of unabashedly imitating good writers so as to improve his own writing. At an early age, he used English essayist Joseph Addison's periodical the *Spectator* as a model, which he systematically tried to duplicate. "I met with an odd volume of the *Spectator*. It was the third. I had never before seen any of them. I bought it, read it over and over, and was much delighted with it. I thought the writing excellent and wished, if possible, to imitate it." His practice was to read an essay, put the periodical aside, and after several days attempt to reproduce the same piece from memory. Later he would compare his own work with the printed material; in so doing he hoped to absorb the style of the original.[31]

For Franklin, one of the most important disciplines was the study of history, a subject he found eminently practical. In fact, he offers an even more thorough rationale for studying history than does Jefferson. He first recommends that more history be incorporated into the study of the Roman and Greek classics so that students might take better advantage of the historical context in which they are studying ancient languages. This approach would be advantageous to the student in part because it would enliven a study that was often tedious. Next, and also like Jefferson, Franklin explains that history is a source of moral teaching. History teaches "morality, by descanting and making continual observations on the causes of the rise or fall of any man's character, fortune, power, etc. mentioned in history; the advantages of temperance, order, frugality, industry, perseverance, etc. etc."[32] Franklin elaborates, "The general natural tendency of reading good history must be to fix in the minds of youth deep impressions of the beauty and usefulness of virtue of all kinds, public spirit, fortitude, etc." Not only will history encourage moral virtue, it will cultivate intellectual virtue as well, since "on historical occasions, questions of right and wrong, justice and injustice will naturally arise, and may be put to youth, which they may debate in conversation and in writing." History, in addition, offers a study in "civil orders and constitutions" so that students can see how political and economic systems have been constructed that have been conducive to, or destructive of, good government.[33]

History is especially useful in promoting one of Franklin's pet interests: the effective use of the English language. To that end, history provides a showcase "of oratory in governing, turning and leading great bodies of mankind, armies, cities, nations." When students are led to admire such elocution, they will be motivated to pursue it themselves, following the models that history provides.

Reiterating his respect for religion, Franklin writes, "History will also afford frequent opportunities of showing the necessity of public religion . . . and the advantage of a religious character among private persons."[34]

Finally, Franklin maintains, the study of history instills in students a desire to study Greek and Latin because of the prominence of those languages in the development of civilization. Here as always, though, Franklin is willing to temper principle with pragmatism by suggesting that not everyone should study ancient languages. Students of divinity must study both Latin and Greek, students of the sciences, Latin, Greek, and French. Law students, though, would better spend their time with Latin and French only, while future merchants need study only modern languages, French, German, and Spanish, ignoring Latin and Greek altogether.[35] (Franklin had taught himself several modern languages, sometimes employing clever strategies to do so. For example, when he and his chess partner were both studying Italian, they agreed that the winner of each match would impose on the loser a drill conducive to improving his mastery of the language.)[36]

We see, then, that Franklin's approach to practical education is characterized by a focus on preparing the individual for private virtue, public civility, and personal success. Woody explains, "It appeared to Franklin inconceivably foolish to educate youth for places in life to which they would not be called. Every word of his educational projects, every practical agency of self and adult education which he founded, had its origin in this principle of practicality." The community, too, would benefit from this practice of educating individuals in the intellectual and moral virtues with a view to their adult success—an approach to social improvement that we might contrast with that of the followers of Dewey, who instead simply coach children to reform their neighborhood upon graduation.[37]

Hence, when we speak of Franklin's educational pragmatism, we mean that his principle interest was in preparing the pupil for

the place for which he was best suited by attending to the development of his character and intellect. This is reminiscent of Plato's
animating educational principle in the *Republic,* in which individuals are prepared for that which nature has equipped them.[38] Franklin's
educational ideas, then, like Jefferson's, implicitly rest upon an acceptance of a natural inequality among students; he certainly does
not advocate an artificially egalitarian scheme.

Franklin was not uninterested in social progress. To the
contrary, with Jefferson he thought educating the individual in virtue to be the surest way of social improvement. Their principles of
education, then, are fundamentally the same, with Franklin laying
emphasis on the organization of a student's education with a view
to his likely livelihood and his willingness to pursue that goal
innovatively. As he explains in *Proposals Relating to the Education of
Youth in Pennsylvania* (1749), the character of the new Pennsylvania
education would be essentially utilitarian precisely because it would
produce individuals of integrity. Its purpose, he writes, is to "supply
the succeeding age with men qualified to serve the public with honor
to themselves, and to their country . . . and to establish young men
in business and other offices."[39]

In Search of Educational Prudence

In the *Politics,* Aristotle notes that "the legislator must . . . make the
education of the young his object above all" and that this "would be
disputed by no one."[40] Although all might agree on the importance
of education, however, this critical undertaking is in need of better
guidance than it presently enjoys. Today, in fact, it often lacks even
the guidance of mere common sense.

In Great Britain, some educational leaders are attempting to
reverse the influences of progressive education on their side of the
Atlantic. One symbol of that influence in Britain is the so-called
Plowden Report of 1967 ("Children and Their Primary Schools"),

which urged schools to embrace progressive teaching and "to abandon traditional, whole-class 'chalk and talk' instruction." After Plowden, phonics and whole-class teaching were dismissed in favor of experimental reading programs and small-group learning. Furthermore, attention to punctuation and grammar was discouraged since such rules allegedly stifled student creativity and initiative. Advocates of these changes drew upon the authority of Dewey and Jean-Jacques Rousseau as well as "research" in support of such changes. However, a later review of poor student performance revealed that the research cited in support of these changes was flimsy. Ensuing investigations linked the poor performance of British students with the prevailing progressive dogmas then reigning in British schools, much of which had been imported from the United States.[41]

Two important conclusions emerged from the British progressive experience. First, there should be caution in using research to justify change. In the British experience, many innovations were supported by a single unpublished dissertation of dubious academic integrity. Second, "progressive orthodoxy" was instituted despite the doubts of many teachers. The British learned that even if a new style of teaching seems to show good results in the "hands of enthusiastic, well-trained staff, it is much less likely to succeed when imposed on those who suspect it and do not understand it."[42]

By the mid-seventies, as scandals erupted over progressive excesses, then prime minister James Callaghan expressed doubts about progressivism. He offered the commonsensical observation that progressive techniques were unreliable, except perhaps in the hands of a few excellent teachers—an observation that could be made of many classroom philosophies and techniques. Progressive reformers often fool themselves in thinking that the narrow experience of a highly enthusiastic teacher with a new method validates a wholly new educational philosophy. Educational historians in Britain have warned, though, that it is not wise to "abandon things that work in the quest for wholesale change."[43]

The kind of common sense that some in Britain are recovering is an expression of the traditional virtue of prudence, or practical wisdom. Practical wisdom, by definition, is the ability to recognize general principles and make sound applications of those principles to everyday practice. Given the counterintuitive practices and counterfactual claims so ubiquitous in education, we might say that what is needed today is a kind of educational prudence, because although educational aspirations abound, sound principles—and commonsensical applications of those principles—are scarce.

Prudence forms a bridge between an abstract principle and its implementation. Since the prudential educational leader must always have an eye to classroom practice, he will be naturally suspicious of unproven pedagogy and will often prevent its precipitous introduction into the classroom. St. Thomas Aquinas explains that prudence is a virtue "most necessary for human life" and is needed because "it matters not only what a man does, but also how he does it." Prudence not only enables one to identify the goal to be achieved—goals like civic education or excellence in mathematics—but also suggests reliable instructional methods conducive to the achievement of such goals.[44]

Those with practical wisdom, according to Aristotle, can see "what is good," and in this light, we appreciate Newman's earlier advice that education should be directed toward the good before anything else, since prudence is essential for the man who wishes to act "with regard to the things that are good or bad."[45] Education will never be *useful* if we consistently craft *bad* policies rather than *good* policies, no matter whether those programs have to do with moral education, reading improvement, or historical literacy. Consistently achieving good teaching policies, then, is impossible without the time-honored quality of practical wisdom.[46]

When formulating curricular plans and pedagogical methods that will have widespread classroom impact, the practically wise individual will take advantage of appropriate counsel and engage in due deliberation. That is, the right people will be involved and the appropriate amount of time will be given to thought and discussion. "Practical wisdom," writes Aristotle, ". . . is concerned with things human and things about which it is possible to deliberate; for we say this is above all the work of the man of practical wisdom, to deliberate well." This suggests that due regard must be given to classroom experience when making decisions, that is, that seasoned teachers are properly involved in policymaking.[47]

Ironically, those who seem to be least consulted by contemporary progressive educational reformers are often the most experienced teachers. This tendency to rush headlong into action is reflective of the young—or at least those youthful in experience. Inexperience, and the rashness that accompanies inexperience, work against the proper functioning of practical wisdom. Accordingly, Aristotle argues that young men in general often lack prudence precisely because of their youth. He explains, "What has been said is confirmed by the fact that while young men become geometricians and mathematicians and wise in matters like these, it is thought that a young man of practical wisdom cannot be found."[48] In other words, if the task involves only abstract thought in the absence of implementation, experience may not be essential. But true prudence comes only with experience.

Alluring theories rather than mundane experience too often drive educational policy. Aristotle, once again, anticipates our error. He suggests that though someone may be unable to offer a theory explaining his classroom methods, he may nonetheless be a very good teacher—perhaps even a reliable guide for those long on theories but short on practice. He writes, "Therefore we ought to attend to the *undemonstrated* sayings and opinions of experienced and older people or of people of practical wisdom not less than to demonstrations [my emphasis]." Though many excellent teachers may be short on "demonstrations" or theories, their "experience has given them an eye [to] see aright." Many a bad educational theory could have been prevented by twenty years—or more—standing in front of students.[49]

Deliberation, moreover, is not the same as research, of which a great deal abounds in education schools today. Such research Aristotle calls "inquiry," which he contrasts with proper deliberation. Deliberation is not the same as "conjecture," which seems better to describe the modern approach to the classroom than deliberation. Stated differently, a lot of careless guesswork is going on. Deliberation, moreover, requires "readiness of mind," which means, among other things, that one is able to discuss educational matters with a mind untainted by irrational prejudice against sound pedagogical ideas and practice.

The dependable exercise of prudence, however, requires even more. Practical wisdom presupposes the sound character and reasonable motives of those who are involved in decision making and implementation. Since the object of prudence is something *good*, then it is necessary that those who try to exercise it do so from reasonably good motives and with generally decent character. Malice or unbridled lust for bureaucratic power will seldom produce sound educational practice. "Practical wisdom," writes Aristotle, "is the quality of mind concerned with things just and noble and good for man, but these are the things which it is the mark of a good man to do." If the aim of practical wisdom is what is good and noble, the bad and ignoble person has no capacity for prudence; indeed, he has no need for it.[50] Both moral virtue and practical wisdom are required on the part of the educational leader; one cannot exist without the other. It is simply "not possible to be good in the strict sense without practical wisdom, or practically wise without moral virtue."[51] Aristotle's principle makes sense: We would not expect the petty or malicious individual to produce reliably good educational programs. To think otherwise contradicts common sense.

Practical wisdom is necessary not only to do good; it is essential if one is to avoid harm. The individual acting without practical wisdom is as likely to damage as to benefit the student. Accordingly, St. Thomas's discussion of practical wisdom comes immediately after his discussion of "folly." Yet we promote untested ideas in the classroom in a way that no dog trainer would attempt in the kennel. Indeed, what better word can we apply to such reckless pedagogy than "folly"? Although some may do foolish things because of an inherent lack of intelligence, St. Thomas Aquinas explains that, more ordinarily, people commit folly by "plunging" headlong into rash activity. Prudence, St. Thomas Aquinas writes, "is the knowledge" not only "of what to seek," but also of "what to avoid."[52]

Finally, if they possessed practical wisdom educational leaders would proceed with due regard for the mystery of the human heart. Blaise Pascal notes, "The heart has its reasons of which reason knows nothing"; and, we might add, contemporary educational research may know nothing of such reasons either.[53] An overly scientific approach to educational success may seduce us into forgetting just how difficult it is to plumb the depths of human behavior, including human learning. The occasional student-perpetrated school massacres that have marred the last decade or more should serve as reminders that we are a long way from describing or understanding the educational process with the precision of the laboratory. Such uncertainty should, at the least, teach us humility and prompt us to obey Pascal's admonition: "Let us then strive to think well."[54]

6

=

Disinheriting Dewey

The devil of Educationism that possesses us is the kind that
can be cast out only by prayer and fasting.
                                    — Flannery O'Connor

WHAT PRACTICAL STEPS MIGHT WE TAKE to disinherit Dewey?
The first consideration for improvement in education is a reiteration of
this book's implication: before undertaking substantial change, it is
imperative to identify the ideas underlying education problems and
proposed reforms. Many disputes in education today are far more than
technical quarrels—they are fundamental philosophical disagreements.
Faced with the current decline in our schools, there is a temptation to
precipitous action, forgetting the Roman dictum *Festina lente* "make
haste slowly." The starting point for any reform must be first to identify
the philosophy at the heart of the problem, and then to ensure that the
ideas behind the solution are sound. Otherwise, reform efforts may be
no more than shadow boxing.

Whenever reform *is* contemplated there emerges an almost irre-
sistible pull back to the ideas of Dewey. For example, after the 1983
report "A Nation at Risk" was published, the Carnegie Foundation
issued its response, "Preparing Teachers for the 21st Century Three Years
Later." The Carnegie report never questioned the hegemony of educa-

tors over education, and it emphasized practices such as "helping students learn to learn" as opposed to specific subject matter.[1]

An important step in this discernment is to distinguish between proposals that represent innovation and those that promote an ideology. As noted in chapter 2, the teaching approach known as "constructivist pedagogy" attempts to pattern a student's learning after the manner in which he himself "constructs" his "own reality." Such a perspective could be helpful in prompting teachers to review and perhaps rejuvenate their teaching styles. But to the extent that "constructivist pedagogy" is a campaign to supplant more traditional teaching philosophies, it may be best defined as an ideological assault rather than a pedagogical method.

Those involved in educational change must define and defend their terms. Words and phrases like "equality," "character," "excellence in education," "critical thinking," "intellectual growth," and the "liberal arts" must be given clear operational definitions. If not, such rhetoric may only offer an appearance of improvement. These terms today mean different things to different people; in some cases they mean little at all. Too many assumptions about terms and concepts have been accepted uncritically. For example, a central progressive assumption, that there is an opposition between "active" learning, which is good; and, "passive" learning, which is bad, may be indefensible. How does a student learn anything if he is not in an active posture? That being true, traditional classrooms have always been populated by "active" learners. To be sure, Dewey's abuse of language for his rhetorical convenience has made it easy to follow the example of Humpty-Dumpty in Lewis Carroll's *Through the Looking Glass*. When Alice complained of his confusing and self-serving vocabulary, he scornfully replied, "When I use a word, it means what I choose it to mean—neither more nor less."[2]

It is past time to adopt a healthy suspicion of experimentation in the classroom, whether those experiments are in the area of sex education, bilingual education, or "exciting new ways" to read and do math. American educators and administrators should adopt the medical profession motto, "First, do no harm." Teachers, the real heroes and heroines in education, are frustrated to the point of tears at having to endure one ill-conceived change after another. Many programs packaged as "better ideas" constitute an impossible burden for instructors. Teachers can survive unruly students, petulant parents, and insufficient funding. Even the best teachers, though, may not long endure the relentless "reforms" imposed upon them from above by their own professions and bureaucracies. It is a wonder that many teach at all; unfortunately, many of the best no longer do, having been driven to despair and resignation.

A frustrated elementary teacher recently observed of the changes imposed on his school: "The maddening thing is that in a few years, all these new requirements will be scrapped in favor of a whole new package of 'better' ideas." The teaching profession is losing teachers, sometimes forcing schools to resort to extreme measures to keep a warm body in the classroom. For the good of both students and teachers, the burden of proof should be on those who want to disrupt learning by introducing "fuzzy math," "whole language," "values clarification" and the like. Parents and teachers should not be in the position of having to constantly assume a defensive posture against an onslaught of "improved" pedagogy.

The scientific method has found a role in the social sciences and education, but it has failed to emerge as the dominant "intelligence" that Dewey promised. Dewey's "one size fits all" use of the scientific method in the classroom to delineate all useful knowledge and human experience is grossly overstated and foolishly misapplied. Faculty at colleges of education too often build careers on peddling innovations to schools, innovations that Dewey might well welcome as "intelligent activity." Indeed, education schools and faculty have at times created small empires sustained by "research" on education, but such research is often of dubious utility—at least to students. Schools seem to teach less well than they did fifty or even a hundred years ago, despite continuous waves of "research-based" innovation. Dewey's legacy is evident in our educational system by the very fact that experimentation has become the unquestioned norm.

Consequently, on the front lines, schools must grapple with fads frequently imposed by the educational bureaucrats to whom they are subordinate. Good books are often replaced by inferior ones simply for the sake of novelty and relevance even though many of these changes make education worse, not better. Schools are regularly thrown into disorder by frequent redesigns of the curriculum, which require the expenditure of scarce resources in order to satisfy administrative dictates. This prevents teachers from attending to the main business of teaching.

To be sure, some in colleges of education are growing aware that their research is irrelevant, but they do not seem to understand why.[3] Not surprisingly, educational researchers often turn to Dewey for help, ignorant of the irony of their plight. One of the most disastrous experiments to be imposed upon students in recent memory is "whole language learning," which has a left a generation of weak readers who are unable to spell. The originators of the program acknowledge Dewey as their inspiration.[4] If true reform is to occur, the Deweyan intellectual heritage must be repudiated, but this could be a measure too painful for many to contemplate since Dewey has supplied the raison d'etre of the educational bureaucracy by his demand for constant experimentation.

This is not meant, however, to discourage innovation, which is by no means the same as experimentation. Innovation builds upon traditional processes and a recognized canon and designs new and dynamic ways to teach that material. Such innovation is important—and appropriate—given the opportunities in computer technology, our growing understanding of the individual needs of certain students, and the opportunities for genuine multiculturalism—properly understood. Progressive experimentation often ignores common sense; innovation incorporates it. In his spiritual autobiography, St. Augustine ruefully wonders why he hated his youthful study of the Greek language.[5] Perhaps if the ancient language had been taught differently he would have had one less reason for self-deprecation later in life.

One can reject Dewey's philosophical baggage yet still pursue innovative teaching. Indeed, the best of educational psychology today demonstrates that an assortment of educational techniques is needed for a variety of learners. In the earlier stages of the progressive movement, some reformers sought to retain traditional educational goals yet pursue those through innovative practices. Such healthy progressive practices, however, were soon overrun by more zealous Dewey-inspired efforts to use classroom innovation as the opportunity to promote radical ideologies. The more extreme such ideas and practices became, the more Dewey sought a public position distinct from these abuses; in reality, such excesses were no more than the faithful implementation of his ideology. For that reason, educational theorists may be well-intentioned but they are wrong when they attempt to exonerate Dewey from the radical expressions of his thought. Though Dewey may not have always liked the implementation of his ideas, he could not explain why such practices were wrong. Richard Hofstadter notes, "Although Dewey himself began to warn in the 1930s against the overuse or the oversimplified use of his theories, he found it difficult to define, even in his later works, the points at which the lines of restraint could or should be drawn without at the same time abandoning certain of his essential commitments."[6]

As a general rule, individual teachers should enjoy the maximum autonomy possible and be rewarded appropriately. The real key to education reform is first philosophical coherence and then excellence in teaching. If teachers are not compensated fairly, fewer talented individuals will pursue teaching careers. Administrators should occasionally rotate back into the classroom to teach for at least a year at a time. They will then be better equipped to serve the teachers, rather than have the teachers serve them.

To be sure, there is the occasional bad apple sitting behind the desk. In these cases, if principals have adequate authority and if parents have proper information, problem teachers may be easier to eliminate. These, however, tend to be the exception; the larger problem is when good teachers are unprepared by irrelevant teacher education programs, crushed under the weight of their own misguided bureaucracy, and unsupported by their own administration. If there were more freedom to teach instead of endless and ever-changing paperwork requirements, veteran teachers might have more time and energy to mentor younger or mediocre teachers, thereby eliminating some of the teaching problems that do exist.[7]

Just as teachers must be freed to do their job, so also must parents be empowered with the maximum choice and discretion possible. They should be involved systematically in their children's education—whether they like it or not. This is not the same, however, as the paternalism that Dewey inspires. Participation should be required if necessary, not in a perfunctory or condescending way, but rather in a principled recognition of the primacy of the parental role.

Vouchers, magnet schools, and charter schools could facilitate such reforms, and public schools would not be destroyed as a result. Indeed, we have accepted a much too narrow definition of the "public." The *good* for society is quality education. If schoolchildren attend a Mennonite or Catholic school, for example, their education is no less "public" than children at the local "public" school. It is just a different way for taxpayers to allocate their money toward the educational good of all. And later, when those Mennonites and Catholics become productive, ethical, patriotic citizens, how will anyone be able to say that the public is not the beneficiary?

It is essential to recapture the beneficial tension once inherent in civic education. On the one hand, citizens should be quick to criticize and correct their government when it is necessary. Accord-

ingly, students should be taught to recognize when government over-
steps its bounds, which means they must study history and government above all. On the other hand, educators are obligated to re-
new the patriotic spirit of the founders in our classrooms, inculcat-
ing in students a sense of civic pride. The eighteenth-century philosopher Montesquieu, whose thought was a major influence on
our founding, explains that a democracy, more than any other type
of government, depends upon its citizens acquiring through education love of one's country. "In republics," Montesquieu insists, "everything depends upon establishing such love."[8] Schools should accordingly follow Lincoln's advice for the aggressive promotion of
the principles, laws, and government of the nation, not just casual
instruction in the social sciences.[9]

This necessarily involves a serious and imaginative study of
history. As Horace Mann explains, "With the wisdom, education
must also teach something of the follies of the past for admonition
and warning; for it has been well said, that mankind [has] seldom
arrived at truth, on any subject, until they had first exhausted its
errors."[10] Technology provides a plethora of creative possibilities for
historical study that teachers should exploit as long as technique
does not trump substance. (And they might keep in mind historian
Barbara Tuchman's advice on how to teach history: "Tell stories.")[11]

Schools must return to their important role of assisting families in forming the moral character of their children by encouraging
virtue. Kant maintains that the "first endeavour in moral education
is the formation of character."[12] Boston College professor William
Kilpatrick observes how common sense once ruled the moral formation of children in schools.

> Teachers understood their main task to be the transmission
> of the culture: passing on to each new generation the les-
> sons—some of them costly—that had been learned about
> right and wrong. In learning right from wrong, young people
> ought to have the benefit of ideas that have been around

for a while. After all, when researchers experiment with new treatments in medicine, the policy is to ask for adult volunteers, not to round up children. Common sense would seem to suggest a similarly cautious approach to experiments in teaching values.[13]

Now, however, educators compete "to outdo one another in rushing the newest developments and techniques into the classroom and into young heads," argues Kilpatrick. Almost overnight we have banished the best ideas from the classroom—"concepts such as virtue, good example, and character formation" have fallen out of favor with educators.[14]

To be sure, over the last decades many initiatives for character education have appeared in our schools. This is an important step in the right direction, even if some of these programs do not take advantage of our philosophical heritage, thereby only promoting a kind of "character lite." To be meaningful, character formation must be based upon a clear notion of individual virtue developed within an unapologetic context of right and wrong, all of which must be drawn from our best philosophical traditions. Many contemporary programs teach students to cultivate character traits for mere utilitarian advantage: "If you are loyal, then your friends will be loyal to you." Students must be taught that virtue is its own reward—even if the consequence of loyalty is personal loss, as it sometimes is. Additionally a young woman should be chaste, not just so that her career is not disrupted by an unwanted pregnancy, but because self-control is the mark of a good person. Self-indulgence is bad not just because it is counterproductive to success; it is bad because it is unworthy of the dignity of a human being. Other programs tend to stress tolerance and self-respect, which although better than teaching intolerance and self-hate, still fall short of the weighty virtues of charity and self-control. Still other schools confuse social conditions—like diversity—with real character traits like patience and benevolence, qualities that alone bring civility to our pluralism.

The contemporary struggle with moral education was predicted several decades ago by philosopher Alasdair MacIntyre in which he asked his reader to suppose a situation in which there occur natural disasters and ensuing social disorder. Consequently, much of the philosophical learning upon which civilization has depended is lost so that only fragmentary knowledge remains. These poorly understood bits of knowledge are used, nonetheless, because this is the only information that citizens still possess. This post-disaster moral literacy, however, is superficial and incoherent even though those involved do not fully realize their handicap. MacIntyre suggests that this is precisely where we are headed—if we are not there already. Indeed, the piecemeal manner in which society is trying to regain a language of character seems to illustrate MacIntyre's thesis. If so, a full recovery of virtue-based education will require our relearning the fundamental moral philosophy we have lost.[15]

We must reaffirm a canon of learning. Dewey's influence is evident, not only in controversies over the subject matter of education, but also in the denial of the possibility of *any* authoritative subject matter. The educational establishment has in large measure accepted the position that no material is important enough to command our respect and to enjoy a fixed status in learning. As we noted in chapter 3, this is the place to which Dewey's reforms have taken us: the annihilation of subject material. The additional problem with this position is that, if the authority of centuries of learning is denied, then authority still must be exercised by someone. In this case, decisions are made by those who happen to hold power in education or by those who have their ear. Surely it is better to trust a body of learning on the basis of centuries of usage than to accept material chosen at the transient whim of an anonymous contemporary "expert" on curricular design. This does not mean that an academic canon must be static; on the contrary, it is a dynamic body of learning open to the accrual of any historical, literary, philosophic, musical, artistic, and scientific subject matter that will enrich humane learning.

In this context, we should note that a major emphasis in school reform today is on "student learning outcomes." Though this idea has rhetorical appeal, it may be misapplied. The first emphasis in education needs to be upon what goes into education, not upon what comes out. In practice, the outcomes approach often means that insufficient attention is given to the substance of education in favor of a preoccupation with measuring arbitrary objectives that may not lend themselves to meaningful analysis, like "civility" or "open-mindedness." In addition, it invites improper experimentation as educators try to reinvent the wheel in order to achieve desired "outcomes"—even if those outcomes are ill defined. The liberal arts have traditionally been most concerned with the actual material to be read and studied; the results of such a curriculum often seem to take care of themselves. As Thomas Jefferson advised his nephew, "Read good books."[16] That should be the first principle of any curriculum.

The current interest in "critical thinking" needs careful examination. There are no shortcuts to analytic and reasoning skills; critical thinking only comes with a well-trained mind. Unfortunately, for too many educators, critical thinking really means the rejection of tradition and the endorsement of the political cause *du jour*. On the other hand, many argue that critical thinking can be learned as nothing more than an isolated skill. Yet, these proponents rarely advocate the traditional disciplines associated with careful thinking: rhetoric and logic. Until they do, critical thinking proposals cannot be taken seriously. Even the pragmatist Charles Peirce ventures that the study of logic is "indispensable."[17]

John Stuart Mill further explains, "Logic is the great disperser of hazy and confused thinking: it clears up the fogs which hide from us our own ignorance, and make us believe that we understand a subject when we do not."[18] He emphasizes the importance of learning the *rules* that govern thinking. The junior and senior years of high school—if not earlier—are suitable for introducing students to informal logic as well as elementary rhetoric. Benjamin Franklin taught himself the basics of logic and rhetoric as a youth, incorporating into that study lessons learned from Xenophon's *Memorable Things of Socrates*.

There is nothing wrong with memorization. It does no violence to a student's creativity to memorize Yeats, nor does it distract her attention from social problems to recite the Gettysburg Address. Indeed, some remedial tutoring companies are turning to rote memorization to toughen the minds of students who have fallen behind. More generally, for the ordinary student, memorization delivers unique cognitive benefits that include strengthening memory, sharpening attentiveness, building language, and absorbing culture.[19]

Once memorization becomes a habit, it is easy to build upon the practice and move to an ever-deepening appreciation of what one has memorized. In doing so, a student takes what he has mastered and interprets it, thus obeying Montaigne's admonition to move beyond more mechanical exercises to consideration and understanding:

> Let the tutor . . . take what the boy has just learned and make him show him dozens of different aspects of it and then apply it to just as many different subjects in order to find out whether he has really grasped it and made it a part of himself . . . Spewing up food exactly as you have swallowed it is evidence of a failure to digest and assimilate it; the stomach has not done its job if, during concoction, it fails to change the substance and the form of what it is given.[20]

Memorizing Shakespeare, to take an example, is also an aid in articulation. Many a phrase learned in high school will provide the *mot juste* years afterward. Today's student needs all the help he can get in self-expression. Recently, a middle school child was interviewed about his harrowing experience on board a cruise ship hit by frightening high waves. After some hesitation, the youngster blurted, "It was just like a movie!"[21]

It is time to euthanize "social studies" and reintroduce the discrete disciplines of history, government, economics, and geography. Prior to the predominance of progressive ideas in the classroom, students typically studied four years of history, including American, European and classical history. Schools also offered courses in government and often geography as well. Since the progressive movement all of those courses have been subsumed under the rubric of social studies. The result has been ambiguous subject matter and vague expectations. Indeed, it is not clear what students should be taught in modern social studies; it is clear, however, that they are not being taught much history, government, economics, or geography.

Social studies courses are often boring and superficial, with only a smattering of history and culture; at worst, social studies material is politicized if not blatantly propagandistic, promoting anti-Western and anti-American dogma. Social studies, moreover, occasionally appear in new and ostensibly exciting garb, most recently with names like "globalization," "internationalization," and "cultural awareness," but this does nothing but conceal in new clothing their frailty and weakness.

The writer Flannery O'Connor was better acquainted than she would have cared to be with the trends of progressive education. She completed a major in "social sciences," but the best thing she could say about her major, she told friends, was that she could remember very little of what she had learned. "I have what passes for an education in this day and time," she writes, "but I am not deceived by it." It is no exaggeration to say that many today are indeed "deceived" by a social studies education, when much richer study in history, geography, government, and economics awaits them.[22]

The concept of "middle school" must be reconsidered. It presently incorporates the flawed premise that middle-school students

cannot be challenged academically as can pupils at other school levels. By design, academic expectations at the middle school level are
low while the push for socializing is high. The teacher's efforts, therefore, are often directed toward "socializing" the pupil, hoping that
parents, teachers, and students alike will survive until high school.
The contemporary middle school evolved out of the junior high
school in the early 1960s and was further radicalized in the late 1980s,
with the socializing mandate growing more intense at each stage.
Author and educator Cheri Yecke asserts that the present socializing
agenda of middle schools is "unethical." She explains, "Public schools
were never meant to be the vehicle for massive social experiments
aimed at achieving the questionable utopian goals of an elite few."[23]
Perhaps the present middle school structure can be kept as long as
the philosophy is changed—but something must give. Middle school
is one of the weakest links in a weak chain.

Middle schools or no middle schools, nearly every level of our
current educational system has discarded the ancient belief that a
liberal education prepares one for the appropriate use of leisure time.
Gone is the Aristotelian-Thomistic view that divides human activity into "work," "play," and "leisure." Whereas we equate leisure
with play or recreation, its etymology reveals another meaning. The
Greek word is *schole*, the root of the word "school." Consistent with
the ideal of liberal education, leisure is the time spent in personal
improvement: moral, intellectual, and spiritual. Work is performed
to provide opportunity for leisure, and play provides relief from
work. Aristotle suggests that the chief priority for the educator is
equipping students to "remain at peace and be at leisure."[24]

There is growing evidence, though, that young people are
helpless when challenged to use their leisure in meaningful ways.
When they experience those rare moments devoid of frenzied activity and multimedia sensory inundation, they apparently plummet
into despair and depression, at least judging by the pervasive ennui
and the self-destructive behavior of America's youth. It is the reac-

tion to just such a "content-free" education that has sparked a renewed interest in the traditional liberal arts education as appropriate formation for any occupational or professional pursuit. The National Endowment of the Arts 2004 report, "Reading at Risk," mentioned in chapter 3, picks up where the landmark study "A Nation at Risk" leaves off:

> "Reading at Risk" reveals an equally dire situation, a culture at risk. The National Endowment for the Arts calls upon public agencies, cultural organizations, the press, and educators to take stock of the sliding literary condition of our country. It is time to inspire a nationwide renaissance of literary reading and bring the transformative power of literature into the lives of all citizens.[25]

Schools, therefore, must work with families in training students to use their leisure time well by helping students establish, among other things, lifelong habits of reading, an objective that necessarily means introducing them to the best literature, music, and art their heritage has to offer.

Colleges of education in general, and the process of teacher formation in particular, must be reintegrated into the major disciplines. Richard Hofstadter explains that after the emergence of isolated teachers colleges within the university at large, "[p]rofessional educators were left to develop their ideas without being subjected to the intellectual discipline that might have come out of a dialogue with university scholars."[26] Consequently, the relationship between "pedagogy" and "content" is out of balance. David McCullough states,

> We have to do a far better job of teaching our teachers. We have too many teachers who are graduating with degrees in education. They go to schools of education or they major in education, and they graduate knowing something called education, but they don't know a subject.[27]

It is widely known that future teachers spend excessive time learning "methods" and "theory," and insufficient time studying the actual disciplines they will teach. A bright education major recently confessed to me that she had to use her electives judiciously outside of her own department, because otherwise she would receive no intellectual stimulation. Colleges of education have forfeited the exclusive control they enjoy over the education of educators. States, likewise, must stop accepting indiscriminately the role of state and national agencies of accreditation. Whatever institutional improvements are made, however, must be pursued with a view to the daunting task of breaking the iron grip of interest groups such as the National Education Association and its state affiliates.

Such a Herculean task, however, can be undertaken only in light of the following principle: education is political and it always will be. Notwithstanding Dewey's disingenuous claim that he stood above partisanship, politics cannot be separated from education any more than it can be removed from any other area of public policy, whether it be welfare, environmental, or foreign policy. The best one can hope for is that the policy struggle be carried out in a civil and statesmanlike manner with all parties identified. As soon as a participant proposes that "politics be set aside," or that those involved should dispense with "labels" like conservative and liberal—as Dewey argues in *Experience and Education* (1938)—the policy-making process becomes dangerous.

Education reform does not involve merely the welfare of students. It is all about gaining and losing power, despite claims to the contrary. There will always be winners and losers, and when we recognize that professional and academic careers are at stake in the struggle over reform, we realize just how big the wins and losses can be. If one does not accept this somber reality, such naiveté may mean that the fight is already lost. As seasoned veterans of U.S. education policy have observed, "Power over our education system has been increasingly concentrated in the hands of a few who don't really want things to change, not substantially, not in ways that would really matter."[28]

The Devil of Educationism

John Dewey had an ambitious political agenda. He compromised the welfare of students for the sake of his opinions and theories and badly damaged the reputation of the American school. It is impossible to determine exactly how much influence Dewey has had on American education, but the parallels between current educational maladies and the most conspicuous features of Dewey's thought make it clear that his influence was large. Yes, the influence of popular culture and the media, the instability of the family, and the waning influence of religion have contributed to educational decline as well. But if it is true that ideas have consequences—and certainly it is—then John Dewey's ideas have been profoundly consequential. The dean of a prominent college of education recently admitted privately, "Education is in a mess and I don't know what we should do. Some days I think we should go back to the one-room schoolhouse and start all over." Indeed, American educators will all remain confused and inert until they recognize and confront the philosophy behind the problems.

In January 2001, President George W. Bush introduced one of the most aggressive federal efforts in education, the "No Child Left Behind" (NCLB) initiative. This intrusive program may create more chaos than real reform. In their compliance efforts, moreover, the states' statistical manipulation has begun to resemble Gogol's wry novel about an enterprising young Russian who purchases "dead souls"—deceased agrarian serfs—so as to make himself appear to have more financial strength than he does.[29] In Detroit, Michigan, and Washington, DC, the debate is about stripping control from local boards of education and handing it to mayors. In 1990 the highest court in Kentucky said the poor quality of the state's classrooms violated the constitutional requirement for an adequate and equal education for all children. The court told the state legislature to "wipe the slate clean." The legislative response was the sweeping Kentucky Education Reform Act.[30] In the Zelman voucher case cited in the preface, the Supreme Court characterized the city of Cleveland as a "failed school district" and noted that a lower court had declared a "crisis of magnitude."[31] Such severe executive, legislative, and judicial intervention is indicative of the seriousness of America's school problem. Without better direction, we should not be surprised to see even more heavy handed measures—for good or ill.

Serious disparities exist in educational funding between schools, and this problem is especially acute when predominately minority and nonminority schools are compared. Indeed, for some, this is the real scandal in education and this inequality demands immediate remedy.[32] The biggest difficulty is the way in which local education is funded, as finances are heavily dependent on property taxes and schools are located in, and tied to, the same neighborhoods where those taxes are levied—thus wealthier districts have better-financed schools. To be sure, equitable school financing is critical but it is even more important to know what and how we should teach. At this point, spending more money to fund Deweyan-inspired schools may provide only better funded Deweyan education—not better education.

G. K. Chesterton notes, "It ought to be the oldest things that are taught to the youngest people." Yet schools are failing to transmit the American intellectual tradition and so are increasingly unable to cope with the present or to anticipate wisely the future.[33] Walter Lippman once observed that "what enables men to know more than their ancestors is that they start with a knowledge of what their ancestors have already learned." "A society," he added, "can be progressive only if it conserves its tradition."[34] Chesterton explains that a society carries "the responsibility of affirming the truth of our human tradition and handing it on with a voice of authority, an unshakable voice." Yet he also notes, "From this high audacious duty the moderns are fleeing on every side; and the only excuse for them is (of course) that their modern philosophies are so half-baked and hypocritical that they cannot convince themselves enough to convince even a new born babe."[35] John Stuart Mill defines education as "the culture which each generation purposely gives to those who are to be its successors, in order to qualify them for at least keeping up, and if possible for raising, the level of improvement which has been attained."[36]

Progressive education appears in many guises. Its animating principle is a rejection of tradition; so that, ironically, *progressive* education is anything but progressive. Despite the rhetoric by which it is promoted, Deweyan-inspired education is not progress *toward* something, it is movement *away* from the best ideas that the Western tradition and human experience have to offer. To be sure, many of the educational thinkers referenced in this volume offer a diversity of views on education, not all of them in agreement. They occupy positions, however, along a continuum. Even if their views are not in harmony, they are complementary, and where complementarity tends to contrast, such differences provide a healthy debate that often leads toward sound and self-critical educational ideas and practices.

Dewey, however, would cast that entire continuum aside and, by the dubious means of experimentation, embark upon the chimerical quest for a wholly new education, a pursuit best distinguished by its opposition to all that has come before. After decades of militant endeavor, he and his many heirs have failed to make such a discovery, so that all the Dewey legacy can offer is scattered monochromatic educational ideas in dull and vague shades of gray. As the English statesman Edmund Burke warns, "[I]t is with infinite caution that any man ought to venture upon pulling down an edifice which has answered in any tolerable degree for ages the common

purposes of society."³⁷ Such a conservative approach to education, moreover, is the surest way to promote change. Hannah
Arendt explains that to *conserve* a school that gives children the
means of *changing* the world is the only revolutionary project
worth pursuing. She argues that education must be "conservative" in order to motivate "what is new and revolutionary in every child."³⁸

What should a good educational philosophy look like? It
should be based upon the wisdom of the ages combined with common sense and empowered by the best innovative practices available. Changing the course of American education will not be easy. It
will take a fight and those so engaged must be morally and intellectually equipped for the task. This fight will take courage, especially
courage understood as Plato explains it, as "a kind of preserving."³⁹
In his "Inaugural Address Delivered to the University of St. Andrews,"
John Stuart Mill insists that a discussion of education "is as fresh to
those who come to it with a fresh mind, a mind not hopelessly filled
full with other people's conclusions."⁴⁰ Horace Mann notes that
education is the most critical activity of any civilized society. He
calls education "that vast cause of which all other causes are dependent, for their vitality and usefulness." He further explains that a
society has as its duty to take "the accumulations in knowledge of
almost six thousand years, and to transfer the vast treasure to pos-
terity." His final point is a warning,

> Suspend its functions for but one generation, and the expe-
> rience and achievements of the past are lost. The race must
> commence its fortunes, anew, and must again spend six
> thousand years, before it can grope its way upward from
> barbarism to the present point of civilization.⁴¹

Given the devastating impact of John Dewey's philosophy in
American education, it is no exaggeration to conclude that we are at
such a historical stage. The decisions we make at this juncture, and

the courage we exhibit, will be the measure of our love for our own children and the generations that follow. A proper education must reject the false conclusion reached by Dewey and his disciples that an education can only be relevant if it is severed from the past. On the contrary, a superficially "modern" education leaves students ill-equipped to deal with the future. As Plato observes, "What is . . . education? Isn't it difficult to find a better one than that discovered over a great expanse of time?"[42] But Plato understates the problem: it is not difficult, but impossible.

Notes

Preface

1. "The data are compelling. We learned in February that American 12th-graders scored near the bottom on the recent Third International Math and Science Study (TIMSS): U.S. students placed 19th out of 21 developed nations in math and 16th out of 21 in science. Our advanced students did even worse, scoring dead last in physics. This evidence suggests that, compared to the rest of the industrialized world, our students lag seriously in critical subjects vital to our future. That's a national shame. . . . Since 1983, more than 10 million Americans have reached the 12th grade without having learned to read at a basic level. More than 20 million have reached their senior year unable to do basic math. Almost 25 million have reached 12th grade not knowing the essentials of U.S. history. And those are the young people who complete their senior year. In the same period, more than 6 million Americans dropped out of high school altogether. The numbers are even bleaker in minority communities. In 1996, 13 percent of all blacks aged 16 to 24 were not in school and did not hold a diploma. Seventeen percent of first-generation Hispanics had dropped out of high school, including a tragic 44 percent of Hispanic immigrants in this age group. . . . Academically, we fall off a cliff somewhere in the middle and upper grades. Internationally, U.S. youngsters hold their own at the elementary level but falter in the middle years and drop far behind in high school. We seem to be the only country in the world whose children fall farther behind the longer they stay in school. That is true of our advanced students and our so-called good schools, as well as those in the middle.

"Remediation is rampant in college, with some 30 percent of entering freshmen (including more than half at the sprawling California State University system) in need of remedial courses in reading, writing, and mathematics after arriving on campus. Employers report difficulty finding people to hire who have the skills, knowledge, habits, and attitudes they require for technologically sophisticated positions. Silicon Valley entrepreneurs press for higher immigration levels so they can recruit the qualified personnel they need. Though the pay they offer is excellent, the supply of competent U.S.-educated workers is too meager to fill the available jobs." See William J. Bennett, Willard Fair, Chester E. Finn Jr., Rev. Floyd Flake, E. D. Hirsch, Will Marshall, Diane Ravitch, et al., "A Nation Still At Risk," *Policy Review* (July-August 1998). Also see Paul Peterson, *Our Schools and Our Future: Are We Still At Risk?* (Stanford, CA: Hoover Institution Press, 2003).

I should note a small minority opinion arguing that the school failure assumption is largely a conspiracy by opponents of public schools. For example Berliner and Biddle describe an "organized malevolence" (xi) behind such "school bashing." (See David C. Berliner and Bruce J. Biddle, *The Manufactured Crisis: Myths, Fraud, and the Attack on America's Public Schools* (New York: Perseus, 1995). This position, though, is held by a very small percentage of scholars and educators. In general, most people, from parents to teachers to administrators, agree that the schools are still very troubled although they may disagree on the cause and on the remedy.

Chapter 1: Dewey's Troubling Legacy

1. Jay Martin, *The Education of John Dewey: A Biography* (Columbia University Press: New York, 2002), 475–77).

2. Just as Dewey's influence on American education is incalculable, so also his foreign influence is considerable. Best known is his reputation in China, but as early 1930, the number of his works translated into other languages was impressive, e.g., French, German, Russian, Hungarian, Arabic, Japanese, and his role was noted in shaping educational reform in Mexico, Germany, Turkey, and England. See Isaac L. Kandel, "John Dewey's Influence on Education in Foreign Lands," in *John Dewey: The Man and His Philosophy* (Cambridge, MA: Harvard University Press, 1930), 65–74.

3. Herbert M. Kliebard, *The Struggle for the American Curriculum: 1893–1995* (New York: Routledge, 1995), xv.

4. Jo Ann Boydston, ed., *John Dewey: The Collected Works, 1882–1953.* (Carbondale, IL: Southern Illinois University Press, 1991). The thirty-seven volumes are also available on CD-ROM. See www.nlx.com/titles/titldewe.htm

5. Sidney Hook, *John Dewey: An Intellectual Portrait* (Amherst, NY: Prometheus, 1995); Alan Ryan, *John Dewey and the High Tide of American Liberalism* (New York: W. W. Norton & Company, 1997); Jennifer Welchman, *Dewey's Ethical Thought* (Ithaca, NY: Cornell University Press, 1995); James Campbell, *Under-*

standing John Dewey: Nature and Cooperative Intelligence. (La Salle, IL: Open Court, 1995); Robert B. Westbrook, *John Dewey and American Democracy* (Ithaca, NY: Cornell University Press, 1991).

6. Larry A. Hickman, ed., *Reading Dewey: Interpretations for a Postmodern Generation* (Bloomington, IN: Indiana University Press, 1998).

7. Alfie Kohn, *The Schools Our Children Deserve* (New York: Houghton Mifflin, 1999).

8. Alfie Kohn, *Beyond Discipline: From Compliance to Community* (Alexandria, Va.: Association for Supervision and Curriculum Development, 1996).

9. Raymond D. Boisvert, *John Dewey: Rethinking Our Time* (Albany, NY: State University of New York Press, 1998).

10. Philip L. Smith, "The Crux of Our Inspiration," *Journal of Genetic Psychology* 155 (September 1994): 355–65.

11. Sara Lawrence-Lightfoot, *The Essential Conversation: What Parents and Teachers Can Learn from Each Other* (New York: Random House, 2003), 249.

12. Phillip C. Schlechty, *Shaking Up the Schoolhouse: How to Support and Sustain Educational Innovation* (San Francisco: Jossey-Bass, 2001), 193.

13. Nicholas O'Hahn, "Inventing the Future, Post 9/11," *Education Week*, October 2, 2002.

14. Kieran Egan, *Getting it Wrong From the Beginning: Our Progressivist Inheritance from Herbert Spencer, John Dewey, and Jean Piaget* (New Haven, CT: Yale University Press, 2002). My primary complaint with this otherwise useful book is that the American "beginning" should refer to the era of the American founding, the leading figures of which were preoccupied with the proper education of the new country, as I discuss in chapter 4.

15. Diane Ravitch, *Left Back: A Century of Battles over School Reform* (New York: Simon and Schuster, 2001). See, for example, 57–59 and 169–79.

16. J. Martin Rochester, *Class Warfare: Besieged Schools, Bewildered Parents, Betrayed Kids, and the Attack on Excellence* (San Francisco: Encounter Books, 2002); and Charles J. Sykes, *Dumbing Down Our Kids: Why American Children Feel Good About Themselves But Can't Read, Write, or Add* (New York: St. Martin's Griffin, 1995).

17. Dewey's more radical philosophical innovations on the liberal experiment cast him farther to the left than others of the same general persuasion. At the same time, as we will see in chapter 4, he supposes that he is the heir to the Jeffersonian tradition. See John Dewey, *Freedom and Culture* (New York: G. P. Putnam's Sons, 1939); and John Dewey, *The Living Thoughts of Thomas Jefferson.* From *The Living Thoughts Library*, ed. Alfred O. Mendel (London: Morrison and Gibb Ltd., 1941).

18. Lawrence A. Cremin, *The Transformation of the School: Progressivism in American Education, 1876–1957*, (New York: Vintage, 1961), 120.

19. Ryan, *John Dewey and the High Tide of American Liberalism,* 253; Westbrook, *John Dewey and American Democracy,* xii; Cremin, *The Transformation of the School,* 237.

20. Hannah Arendt, *Essays in Understanding, 1930–1954: Formation, Exile, and Totalitarianism* Jerome Kohn, ed. (New York: Harcourt Brace, 1994), 194.

21. Quoted in David Fott, *John Dewey: America's Philosopher of Democracy* (Lanham, MD: Rowman and Littlefield, 1998), 21.

22. *Leo R. Ward,* Moral Philosophy, *chap. 14, located at www.nd.edu/Departments/ Maritain/etext/jmoral14.htm.*

23. Leo R. Ward, "John Dewey in Search of Himself," *Review of Politics* 19 (April 1957): 205–13.

24. Many illustrations could be offered. See, for example, Douglas Simpson and Michael Jackson, *Educational Reform: A Deweyan Perspective* (New York: Garland Publishing, 1997); Laurel Tanner, *Dewey's Laboratory School: Lessons for Today* (New York: Teachers College Press, 1997); Stephen Fishman and Lucille McCarthy, *John Dewey and the Challenge of Classroom Practice* (New York: Teachers College Press, 1998).

25. Westbrook, *John Dewey and American Democracy,* 168.

26. George Dykhuizen, *The Life and Mind of John Dewey* (Carbondale, IL: Southern Illinois University Press, 1973), 180.

27. Ryan, *John Dewey and the High Tide of American Liberalism,* 186.

28. Westbrook, *John Dewey and American Democracy,* 290–91.

29. Dykhuizen, *The Life and Mind of John Dewey,* 207.

30. Ryan, *John Dewey and the High Tide of American Liberalism,* 31.

31. Dewey, incidentally, also proclaims the need for a "Copernican revolution" in his short text *The School and Society* (1899). In keeping with the astronomy metaphor, he explains that the "center of gravity" of the school needs to shift to the student and away from the teacher and textbook (SS, 51).

32. Fott, *John Dewey,* 29.

33. Martin, *The Education of John Dewey,* 492.

34. Ibid., 482.

35. Michel de Montaigne, *The Complete Essays,* trans. M. A. Screech (London: Penguin, 1991), 1212, 1211.

Chapter 2: A New Way to Be Human

1. Relevant to Dewey's attitude toward religion may be Dewey's mother Lucinda's overbearing Congregationalism, the effect of which, we might suppose, was to later backfire with Dewey's hostility to conventional religious practice. Dewey

himself called it a "trying personal crisis" (quoted in Richard Bernstein, *John Dewey* [Atascadero, California: Ridgeview Publishing Company, 1981], 160). This is the conclusion that Steven C. Rockefeller draws in *John Dewey: Religious Faith and Democratic Humanism* (New York: Columbia University Press, 1991), 38, 559. Some have dignified Dewey's lack of faith by calling attention to his belief in natural experience, thus pointing to his "natural piety" (see, e.g., Bernstein, 162). This is the essential thesis of Rockefeller's attempt to bring respectability to Dewey's aggressive secularism by redefining the traditional meaning of religious faith. Some, though, might consider terms like "natural piety" or "natural religion" euphemisms for atheism, especially as they are applied to Dewey's radical secularism. Throughout his writing career, however, Dewey cannot resist religious imagery such as the "narrow path." At one point, he even compares himself, in passing, to John the Baptist (see Rockefeller, *John Dewey*, 326). Elsewhere, Dewey wistfully predicts that his new educational science will lead us into the "promised land" (RP, 28); in another place he offers a "gospel" of present growth (HNC, 284).

2. John Dewey, introduction to Corliss Lamont, *The Illusion of Immortality* (New York: Continuum, 1990), xiii.

3. *John Dewey: The Political Writings*, ed. Debra Morris and Ian Shapiro (Indianapolis: Hackett Publishing, 1993), 248.

4. "Humanist Manifesto I," located at www.americanhumanist.org/about/manifesto1.html.

5. John Dewey, "The Logic of Judgments of Practice," in *John Dewey: The Middle Works, 1899–1924*, vol. 8, 59.

6. Gilbert T. Sewall, "The Postmodern Schoolhouse," in *Dumbing Down: Essays on the Strip-Mining of American Culture*, ed. Datherine Washburn and John Thornton (New York: W. W. Norton & Company, 1996), 66.

7. John Dewey, preface to *How We Think* (Mineola, NY: Dover, 1997).

8. Although in *Human Nature and Conduct*, Dewey only makes vague allusions to Rousseau's ideas, in *Schools of Tomorrow* (1915), as we shall see, Dewey unabashedly embraces and endorses Rousseau's educational views.

9. Even Dewey's supporters cannot save him from the confusion that his terminology generates. Attempts to rescue him by means of "clarifications" seem to make matters worse. For example, Cuffaro writes, "Over the decades, Dewey used the words *interaction* and *transaction* interchangeably just as the words *disposition, character*, and *attitude* became other names for habit in many of his writings." Harriet K. Cuffaro, *Experimenting with the World: John Dewey and the Early Childhood Classroom* (New York: Teachers College Press, 1995), 24. Another example of this terminological carelessness appears in *Experience and Education* when he redefines the human soul as a "quality" of "psycho-physical activities," 293.

10. Jaime Castiello, *A Humane Psychology of Education,* 8–9.

11. Rochester, *Class Warfare,* xx.

12. James Davison Hunter, *The Death of Character: Moral Education in an Age without Good and Evil* (New York: Basic Books, 2000), xv.

13. The goal of values clarification is not to create a virtuous young person or young adult with character or probity; its goal is to empower youngsters to make their own decisions, whatever those decisions might be. The authors of the handbook explain that their curriculum "is based on the approach formulated by Louis Raths, who in turn built upon the thinking of John Dewey." Noted in Sykes, *Dumbing Down Our Kids,* 162. Also see Sidney B. Simon, *Values Clarification: A Handbook of Practical Strategies for Teachers and Students* (New York: Hart Publishing, 1972), 15.

14. John Dewey, *The Quest for Certainty* (New York: Minton, Balch & Company, 1929), 277.

15. Evan Keliher, "Forget the Fads—The Old Way Works Best," *Newsweek,* September 30, 2002, 18.

16. Martin, *The Education of John Dewey,* 55. Also see Dykhuizen, *The Life and Mind of John Dewey,* 24. Dykhuizen's characterization of Dewey's teaching in Charlotte is similar. Even an ardent admirer like Sydney Hook admitted that Dewey's teaching—this time at the college level—was so uninspired as to violate "his pedagogical principles" (quoted in Ryan, *John Dewey and the High Tide of American Liberalism,* 38).

17. Ryan, *John Dewey and the High Tide of American Liberalism,* 38.

18. David Fott is one of the few who seriously (if briefly) discusses the Nietzschean impulse in Dewey's thought. See his *John Dewey,* 114ff, 99. Also see Paul K. Crosser, *The Nihilism of John Dewey* (New York: Philosophical Library, 1955).

19. Dewey was well acquainted with Nietzsche's writing, at least from the time of his graduate education. In the context of a general discussion of freedom in *Freedom and Culture* (1939), he mentions Nietzsche and in so doing defends the German philosopher from criticism Dewey thinks is unfair. Dewey notes that "some writers, notably Nietzsche (though not in the crude form often alleged) proposed an ethics of power in opposition to the supposed Christian ethics of sacrifice" (17). There are even a few passages in Dewey's writing that appear to be quotes or paraphrases from Nietzsche's writing, although Dewey incorporates the passages without attribution. It is interesting as well that Dewey blamed Kant for Germany's twentieth-century moral disaster but declines to indict Nietzsche for the same. See John Dewey, "German Philosophy and Politics," in *John Dewey: The Middle Works, 1899–1924,* vol. 8, 151.

20. Friedrich Nietzsche, *Beyond Good and Evil: Prelude to a Philosophy of the Future,* trans. Walter Kaufmann (New York: Vintage, 1966). I find it noteworthy that in the introductory essay to volume 4 of Dewey's *Middle Works,* Wayne A. R.

Leys asserts that as early as the 1890s, Dewey was, in his approach to ethics, "committed to 'going beyond conventional right and wrong' as surely as Nietzsche . . . had gone 'beyond good and evil.'" Leys, however, does try to save Dewey from too close an association with Nietzsche, going so far as to suggest that Dewey, during this period of his intellectual life, "had apparently not read Nietzsche," a claim I frankly don't understand. *John Dewey: The Early Works, 1882–1898,* vol. 4, xxiv.

21. Napoleon is also cited conspicuously by Nietzsche as an illustration of "genius." Here as elsewhere, Dewey seems to have Nietzsche's text in mind as he crafts his own prose even if he does not acknowledge Nietzsche. See Friedrich Nietzsche, *Twilight of the Idols,* trans. Richard Polt (Indianapolis: Hackett Publishing, 1997), 78.

22. Saito, Naoko, "Pragmatism and the Tragic Sense: Deweyan Growth in an Age of *Nihilism,*" *Journal of the Philosophy of Education* 36 (May 2002): 247–64. A review of the leading educational academic journals reveals a startling strong interest in Nietzsche's ideas and their possible relevance for, and application to, educational practice. See, for example, Stefan Ramaekers, "Teaching to Lie and Obey: Nietzsche on Education," *Journal of Philosophy of Education* 35 (May 2001): 255–68; Charles Bingham, "What Friedrich Nietzsche Cannot Stand About Education: Toward A Pedagogy of Self-Reformulation," *Educational Theory* 51 (summer 2001): 337–52; Haim Gordon, "Nietzsche's Zarathustra as Educator," *Journal of Philosophy of Education* 14, no. 2 (1980): 181–92; David Cooper, "On Reading Nietzsche on Education," *Journal of Philosophy of Education* 17, no. 1 (1985): 119–26; A. M. Sharp, "Nietzsche's View of Sublimation in the Educational Process," *Journal of Educational Thought* 9, no. 2 (1984): 99–106; Eliyahu Rosenow, "What is Free Education? The Educational Significance of Nietzsche's Thought," *Educational Theory* 23, no. 4 (1973): 354–70; James Hillesheim, "Nietzsche Agonistes," *Educational Theory* 23, no. 4 (1973): 343–53; Aloni Nimrod, "The Three Pedagogical Dimensions of Nietzsche's Philosophy," *Educational Theory* 39, no. 4 (1989): 305–6.

23. Friedrich Nietzsche, "Thus Spoke Zarathustra," in *The Portable Nietzsche,* Walter Kaufmann, ed. (New York: Penguin Books, 1986), 171.

24. Two of the seminal books in this movement are Louis E. Raths, Merrill Harmin, and Sidney Simon, *Values and Teaching: Working with Values in the Classroom* (Columbus, OH: C. E. Merrill Books, 1966); and Sidney Simon, *Values Clarification.*

25. Hunter, *The Death of Character,* 182.

Chapter 3: Dewey's Revolt

1. Dewey's fullest discussion of his instrumental approach to aesthetics is found in *Art as Experience* (New York: Minton, Balch & Co., 1934).

2. Diane Ravitch, *The Language Police: How Pressure Groups Restrict What Students Learn* (New York: Alfred A. Knopf, 2003).

3. Sec. 102 H.R. 1804, "Goals 2000: Educate America Act." http://www.ed.gov/legislation/GOALS2000/TheAct/index.html

4. *An Invitation to Your Community: Building Community Partnerships for Learning: Goals 2000, A World Class Education for Every Child*, U.S. Department of Education, January 1995. The quote, by President Clinton, is prominently placed on the front cover of the pamphlet. It is also worth noting that the cover illustration pictures a number of people forming a ring around a schoolhouse. None of these individuals, however, can be clearly identified as a parent.

5. Frederick Douglass, *Life and Times of Frederick Douglass* (New York: Collier Books, 1962), 84.

6. This particular discussion occurs in the context of the "Gary Plan," as it was known, which came to a "ruinous" end in New York City, where, in an attempt to implement the program on a widespread basis, it was caught in the crossfire of local education politics and abandoned. See Sarah Mondale and Sarah B. Patton, eds., *School: The Story of American Education* (Boston: Beacon Press, 2001), 68.

7. See www.nea.gov/pub/ReadingAtRisk.pdf.

8. Richard Hofstadter, *Anti-intellectualism in American Life* (New York: Alfred A. Knopf, 1964), 373.

9. Ryan, *John Dewey and the High Tide of American Liberalism*, 163.

10. Fott, *John Dewey*, 151.

11. Martin, *The Education of John Dewey*, 429.

12. Making sense of Dewey's thought on goals, standards, aims, and objectives is an especially frustrating task. I would refer again to Leo Ward's essay in which he enumerates several of the conspicuous contradictions in Dewey's thought in this area. See "John Dewey in Search of Himself," 205–13.

13. Dykhuizen, *The Life and Mind of John Dewey*, 78.

14. Cremin, *The Transformation of the School*, 176.

15. Ryan, *John Dewey and the High Tide of American Liberalism*, 277.

16. Kliebard, *The Struggle for the American Curriculum*, 202.

17. Another similar work by Dewey during this time, although shorter and more superficial, is his *The Way Out of Educational Confusion* (Cambridge, MA: Harvard University Press, 1931).

18. For example, see Bernstein, *John Dewey*, 71.

19. In this light, it is instructive to note the leading Deweyan Alfie Kohn's *The Schools Our Children Deserve*. Kohn's thought is not only a contemporary presentation of Dewey's ideas; his rhetoric, unfortunately, is marred, as is Dewey's, by careless logic and polarizing contemptuous phrases about traditional practices such as "drill 'n kill," "deadly book reports," "Drop Everything And Drill (DEAD)," and "the Old School manages to screw up . . ." In traditional schools, moreover, students "are lectured at" and must "slog along."

20. Martin, *The Education of John Dewey*, 493.

Chapter 4: Democracy Betrayed

1. See nces.ed.gov/pressrelease/rel2002/5_9_02.asp.

2. See www.ed.gov/news/speeches/2002/05/05092002.html.

3. "History Failure: Doomed to Repeat Itself?" located at edreform.com/pubs/history.htm.

4. See www.education-world.com/a_issues/issues100.shtml.

5. "Students Flunk U.S. History Test: Congress Calls on Teachers to 'Redouble Efforts,'" located at www.educationworld.com/a_issues/issues100.shtml.

6. Mona Charen, "Don't Know Much About History," located at www.jewishworldreview.com/cols/charen071503.asp.

7. For examples of those who erroneously regard Dewey and Jefferson's ideas as harmonious, see Rosemary C. Salamone, "Education for Democratic Citizenship," *Education Week*, March 22, 2000; Katherine G. Simon, "Making Room for Moral Questions in the Classroom," *Education Week*, November 7, 2001; and Freda Schwartz, "Reading, 'Righting, Reacting," *Education Week*, May 16, 2001. Dewey scholar Milton R. Koonvitz, by contrast, exposes Dewey's dramatic departure from Jefferson, noting that Dewey thought Jefferson's ideas "pathetically inadequate"; however, he justifies Dewey's revision of Jefferson as constituting genuine progress in educational thought. See his "Dewey's Revision of Jefferson," in *John Dewey: Philosopher of Science and Freedom*, ed. Sidney Hook (New York: Barnes & Noble, 1950), 164–76.

8. Charles Finn Arrowood, ed., *Thomas Jefferson and Education in a Republic* (New York: McGraw-Hill, 1930), 52.

9. Roy J. Honeywell, *The Educational Work of Thomas Jefferson* (Cambridge, MA: Harvard University Press, 1931).

10. Ibid., 148, 242.

11. Eva T. H. Brann, *Paradoxes of Education in a Republic* (Chicago: University of Chicago Press, 1979), 52–57.

12. Harvey Mansfield Jr., "Thomas Jefferson" in *American Political Thought: The Philosophic Dimension of American Statesmanship*, ed. Morton J. Frisch and Richard G. Stevens (New York: Charles Scribner's Sons, 1971), 38.

13. Daniel Boorstin, *The Lost World of Thomas Jefferson* (Boston: Henry Holt, 1948), 145.

14. Merrill D. Peterson, *The Portable Thomas Jefferson* (New York: Penguin, 1988), 425.

15. Ibid.

16. Lorraine Smith Pangle and Thomas L. Pangle, *The Learning of Liberty: The Educational Ideas of the American Founders* (Lawrence, KS: University Press of Kansas, 1993), 122.

17. Honeywell, *The Educational Work of Thomas Jefferson*. Also see Arrowood, *Thomas Jefferson and Education in a Republic*.

18. See David B. Tyack, "Forming the National Character: Paradox in the Revolutionary Thought of the Founding Generation," in *Turning Points in American Educational History* (Waltham, MA: Blaisdell Publishing Co., 1967), 83–118.

19. Peterson, *The Portable Thomas Jefferson*, 393.

20. Tyack, "Forming the National Character," 86.

21. See speaker.house.gov/library/texts/lincoln/lyceum1.asp.

22. Honeywell, *The Educational Work of Thomas Jefferson*, 199. Also see John C. Walton and Alma H. Preinkert, "The Educational Views of George Washington, Based on His Letters, Diaries, and Addresses," in *The History of the George Washington Bicentennial Celebration*, vol. 1 (Washington, DC: U.S. George Washington Bicentennial Commission, 1932), 543.

23. Peterson, *The Portable Thomas Jefferson*, 197–98.

24. Pangle and Pangle, *The Learning of Liberty*, 111; Peterson, *The Portable Thomas Jefferson*, 197–98.

25. Kliebard, *The Struggle for the American Curriculum*, 124–28.

26. Pangle and Pangle, *The Learning of Liberty*, 111.

27. Brann, *Paradoxes of Education in a Republic*, 81.

28. Noted in Ryan, *John Dewey and the High Tide of American Liberalism*, 325.

29. Mansfield, "Thomas Jefferson," 23.

30. Adrienne Koch, *Power, Morals, and the Founding Fathers: Essays in the Interpretation of the American Enlightenment*, (Ithaca, NY: Great Seal Books, 1961), 45–46.

31. Mansfield, "Thomas Jefferson," 37–38.

32. Martin, *The Education of John Dewey*, 383.

33. Hook, *John Dewey*, 230.

34. Martin, *The Education of John Dewey*, 354.

35. Ibid., 356.

36. Westbrook, *John Dewey*, 478.

37. Martin, *The Education of John Dewey*, 392.

38. A recent example of such an interpretation is found in Kohn's *Beyond Discipline*.

39. Emblematic of this faith in "communication" is the guide to education reform noted in chapter 1, *The Essential Conversation*, by Sara Lawrence-Lightfoot.

40. Rochester, *Class Warfare*, 126.

41. Allan Bloom, *The Closing of the American Mind: How Higher Education Has Failed Democracy and Impoverished the Souls of Today's Students* (New York: Simon and Schuster, 1988), 56.

42. Bloom, *The Closing of the American Mind*, 29.

Chapter 5: A Useful Education

1. J. R. R. Tolkien, "Leaf by Niggle," in *The Tolkien Reader* (New York: Ballantine Books, 1966), 119

2. J. R. R. Tolkien, *The Hobbit, or There and Back Again* (New York: Ballantine Books, 1937, 1997), 62.

3. Aristotle, *Politics*, trans. Carnes Lord (Chicago: University of Chicago Press, 1984), 1337a139–40.

4. John Henry Newman, *The Idea of a University*, ed. Frank M. Turner (New Haven, CT: Yale University Press, 1996), 118

5. Ibid; Newman's italics.

6. Ibid., 125–26.

7. Ibid.

8. Ibid., 117.

9. Aristotle, *Politics*, 1332b1:15–1334a1:25.

10. Castiello, *A Humane Psychology of Education*, 138

11. Ibid., 137–38.

12. Aristotle, *Politics*, 1276b1:15–30.

13. Ibid., 1332a1:19–20.

14. Horace Mann, "Lecture on Education," in *From Plato to Piaget: The Greatest Educational Theorists from Across the Centuries and Around the World*, ed. William Cooney, Charles Cross, Barry Trunk (Lanham, MD: University Press of America, 1993), 95–103.

15. Aristotle, *Nichomachean Ethics*, trans. David Ross (Oxford: Oxford University Press, 1984), 1102a14.

16. Ibid., 1094b12–1095a6.

17. For example, see, Mary E. Huba and Jan E. Freed, *Learner-Centered Assessment on College Campuses: Shifting the Focus from Teaching to Learning* (Boston: Allyn and Bacon, 1999).

18. Aristotle, *De Anima* (London, Penguin, 1986), 402a.

19. Plato, *Republic*, trans. Allan Bloom (Philadelphia: Basic Books, 1968), 444e.

20. Plutarch, *Moralia*, in *Classics in Education*, ed. Wade Baskin (New York: Philosophical Library, 1966), 555.

21. J. R. R. Tolkien, *The Return of the King* (Boston: Houghton Mifflin, 1991), 915.

22. Aristotle, *Metaphysics* (Grinnell, IA: Peripatetic Press, 1979), 980a.

23. "On Educating Children," in Montaigne, *The Complete Essays*, 199.

24. Thomas Woody, ed., *Educational Views of Benjamin Franklin* (New York: McGraw-Hill, 1931), 103–9.

25. Benjamin Franklin, *The Private Life of the Late Benjamin Franklin, LL.D.*, chap. 8, located at www.earlyamerica.com/lives/franklin/chapt8/index.html.

26. Woody, *Educational Views of Benjamin Franklin*, 55.

27. Ibid., 41.

28. Ibid., 64, 87–88.

29. Ibid., 91; Franklin, *The Private Life of the Late Benjamin Franklin*, chap. 8.

30. Woody, *Educational Views of Benjamin Franklin*, 132–33.

31. Franklin, *The Private Life of the Late Benjamin Franklin*, chap. 1; Woody, *Educational Views of Benjamin Franklin*, p. 41.

32. Woody, *Educational Views of Benjamin Franklin*, 168.

33. Ibid., 170–71.

34. Ibid., 168–79, 173.

35. Ibid.

36. Franklin, *The Private Life of the Late Benjamin Franklin*, chap. 9.

37. Woody, *Educational Views of Benjamin Franklin*, 109.

38. Plato, *Republic*, 419a–445e.

39. Woody, *Educational Views of Benjamin Franklin*, 142.

40. Aristotle, *Politics*, 1337a1.

41. The progressive British movement is, for many, symbolized by Summerhill School in Suffolk County, founded by A. S. Neill in 1921. The school, where classes are still optional, has been a symbol for many of the worst in British progressive education. A description of the Summerhill School can be found at www.summerhillschool.co.uk/indexgo.html.

42. "Plowden's Progress," *Economist,* July 18, 1998

43. "Plowden's Progress," *Economist,* July 18, 1998; Maurice Galton, *Crisis in the Primary Classroom* (London: David Fulton Publishers, 1994). For a biting indictment of the damage inflicted on British students—especially boys—by progressive education, see Janet Daley, "Progressive Ed's War on Boys," in *City Journal* (winter 1999). For a positive view of progressive education in Britain, see "Bethan Marshall: Jamie's a Good Teacher, Too," March 31 2005, *Independent*, located at education.independent.co.uk/schools/story.jsp?story=624934.

44. Thomas Aquinas, *Summa Theologica*, II-II, qu. 57, a. 3-5.
45. Aristotle, *Nichomachean Ethics*, 1140a20ff; 1140b6ff.
46. Ibid., 1141b33ff.
47. Ibid.
48. Ibid., 1142a7ff..
49. Ibid., 1143a31.
50. Ibid., 1143b18ff.
51. Ibid., 1143b35; 1144b29.
52. Thomas Aquinas, *Summa Theologica*, II-II, qu. 46, a. 1; qu. 47
53. Blaise Pascal, *Pensées*, trans. A. J. Krailsheimer (London: Penguin, 1995), no. 200, no. 423.
54. Ibid.

Chapter 6: Disinheriting Dewey

1. *A Nation Prepared: Teachers for the 21st Century: The Report of the Task Force on Teaching as a Profession* (New York: Carnegie Foundation, 1986).
2. Lewis Carroll, *Alice in Wonderland*, ed. Donald J. Gray (New York: W. W. Norton & Company, 1971), 163. For a revealing article on the misuse of language in education, see
Linda Perlstein, "Talking the Edutalk: Jargon Becoming Prevalent in the Classroom," *Washington Post*, January 18, 2004, A1.
3. See, for example, Debra Viadero, "Scholars Aim to Connect Studies to Schools' Needs," *Education Week*, March 19, 2003.
4. The literature is extensive and the Dewey influence is patent. See, for example, Gordon Wells, *The Meaning Makers: Children Learning Language and Using Language to Learn* (Portsmouth: Heinemann, 1985); Yetta Goodman, "Roots of the Whole-Language Movement," *Elementary School Journal* 90, no. 2 (November 1989): p. 113-27; Kenneth S. Goodman, "Whole-Language Research: Foundations and Development," *Elementary School Journal* 90, no. 2 (November 1989): 207–21; Pamela S. Carroll, "John Dewey for Today's Whole Language Middle School," *Middle School Journal* 26, no. 3, January 1995, 62–68; Norman Weston and John H. Ingram, "Whole Language and Technology: Opposites, or Opposites in Harmony?" *Educational Horizons* 75, no. 2 (winter 1997): 83–89; Betty Jane Wagner, "Whole Language: Integrating the Language Arts—and Much More," *ERIC Digest*, ED313675, 1989, located at www.ericdigests.org/pre=9213/whole.htm.
5. Augustine, *Confessions*, bk. 1, chap. 23, located at www.catholicfirst.com/thefaith/catholicclassics/staugustine/confessions01.cfm.

6. Hofstadter, *Anti-Intellectualism in American Life*, 368.

7. For just one example of the contemporary plight of teachers, see Daniel Moulthrop, Nínive Clements Calegari, and Dave Eggers, *Teachers Have It Easy: The Big Sacrifices and Small Salaries of America's Teachers* (New York: New Press, 2005).

8. Montesquieu, *Selected Political Writings*, trans. Melvin Richter (Indianapolis: Hackett Publishing Company, 1990), 138–39.

9. See speaker.house.gov/library/texts/lincoln/lyceum1.asp.

10. Mann, "Lecture on Education," in *From Plato to Piaget: The Greatest Educational Theorists From Across the Centuries and Around the World*, William Cooney et al., eds. (Lanham, MD: University Press of America, 1993), 96.

11. David McCullough, "Acceptance Speech," located at www.nationalbook.org/ nbaacceptspeech_dmccullough.html.

12. Immanuel Kant, *Education* (Ann Arbor, MI: University of Michigan Press, 1960), 84.

13. William Kilpatrick, *Why Johnny Can't Tell Right From Wrong: And What We Can Do About It* (New York: Touchstone, 1992), 78.

14. Ibid., 79.

15. Alasdair MacIntyre, *After Virtue* (Notre Dame, IN: University of Notre Dame Press, 1984), 1–2.

16. Peterson, *The Portable Thomas Jefferson*, 425.

17. Charles Peirce, "The Function of a University," in *Classics in Education*, ed. Wade Baskin (New York: Philosophical Library, 1966), 512. See also Franklin, *The Private Life of the Late Benjamin Franklin,* chap. 1.

18. John Stuart Mill, "Inaugural Address," in *Essays on Equality, Law, and Education*, ed. John M. Robson and Stefan Collini (Toronto: University of Toronto Press), 239.

19. There is a growing awareness that progressive education has undermined the school habit of memorization, which was a regular practice until the 1970s. See for example, Michael Knox Beran, "In Defense of Memorization," *City Journal* (summer 2004), located at www.city-journal.org/html/ 14_3_defense_memorization.html; and Carol Muske Dukes, "A Lost Eloquence," New York Times, December 29, 2002, located at www.carolmuskedukes.com/articles/2002_articles/NYTimesOPEDdec02.htm. As one retired school teacher sardonically explains, "Today's professionalized, bureaucratized, consolidated systems of schools shun memorization of poetry. A stronger signal of the value of the practice we could not have" (www.educationnews.org/reclaiming-a-literary-heritage.htm).

20. Montaigne, "On Educating Children," 169

21. This was reported on Fox News on April 19, 2005, in regard to the cruise ship *Norwegian Dawn* incident on April 16, 2005, off the coast of South Carolina.

22. Flannery O'Connor, *The Habit of Being* (New York: Farrar, Straus & Giroux, 1979), 68.

23. See www.townhall.com/bookclub/yecke.html.

24. Aristotle, *Politics*, 1331b1:25–1332b1.

25. See www.nea.gov/pub/ReadingatRisk.pdf.

26. Hofstadter, *Anti-intellectualism in American Life*, 338.

27. David McCullough, "Knowing History and Knowing Who We Are," *Imprimis* 34, no. 4 (April 2005).

28. William J. Bennett, Willard Fair, Chester E. Finn Jr., Floyd Flake, E. D. Hirsch, Will Marshall, Diane Ravitch et al., "A Nation Still At Risk," *Policy Review* (July–August 1998), no. 90.

29. For example, see, Marie Gryphon, "Education Law Encourages Fuzzy Math," February 28, 2005, at www.cato.org/pub_display.php?pub_id=3694; also Nikolai Gogol, *Dead Souls* (New York: Vintage, 1997).

30. Holly Holland Portsmouth, *Making Change: Three Educators Join the Battle for Better Schools* (Portsmouth, NH: Heinemann, 1998), x.

31. See supct.law.cornell.edu/supct/html/00-1751.ZS.html.

32. See, for example, the writings of Jonathan Kozol.

33. American Council of Trustees and Alumni, *To Reclaim a Legacy: A Report on the Humanities in Higher Education,* located at www.higher-ed.org/resources/legacy.htm.

34. Quoted in Kilpatrick, *Why Johnny Can't Tell Right From Wrong,* 79.

35. G. K. Chesterton, *What's Wrong with the World,* vol. 4 in *Collected Works* (Ft. Collins: Ignatius Press, 1986), 167.

36. Mill, "Inaugural Address," 217.

37. Edmund Burke, *Reflections on the Revolution in France,* ed. J. G. A. Pocock (Indianapolis, Hackett Publishing Company, 1787), 53.

38. Hannah Arendt, "The Crisis in Education," in *Between Past and Future* (New York: Viking, 1961), 193.

39. Plato, *Republic,* 429c–d.

40. Mill, "Inaugural Address," 217.

41. Mann, "Lecture on Education," 95–96.

42. Plato, *Republic*, 376e.

Index

About the Author

Henry (Hank) T. Edmondson III is Professor of Political Science at Georgia College, the state's public liberal arts university. In 2003 he received the university's highest award, that of distinguished professor, for excellence in teaching, research, and university service. He has lectured in the U.S. and Europe on educational philosophy and reform and he has written widely on a variety of topics, including education, ethics, Shakespeare, J. R. R. Tolkien, and Flannery O'Connor. A consultant with the Georgia Department of Education, his books include *Return to Good and Evil: Flannery O'Connor's Response to Nihilism* and (as editor) *The Moral of the Story: Literature and Public Ethics*.